WHY JESUS?

NAVIGATING HIS TRANSFORMATIVE MESSAGE

Unveiling the Timeless Impact of His Word

❦

KARYN LEE CHUA

Ark House Press
arkhousepress.com

Scriptures taken from the Holy Bible, New International Version®, NIV®. Copyright © 1973, 1978, 1984, 2011 by Biblica, Inc.™ Used by permission of Zondervan. All rights reserved worldwide. www.zondervan.com The "NIV" and "New International Version" are trademarks registered in the United States Patent and Trademark Office by Biblica, Inc.™

Scripture taken from the New King James Version®. Copyright © 1982 by Thomas Nelson. Used by permission. All rights reserved.

Cataloguing in Publication Data:
Title: Why Jesus? Navigating His Transformative Message
ISBN: 978-0-6459938-6-8 (pbk)
Subjects: REL012040 [RELIGION / Christian Living / Inspirational]; REL012120 [RELIGION / Christian Living / Spiritual Growth]; REL030000 [RELIGION / Christian Ministry / Evangelism]

Design by initiateagency.com

CONTENTS

RESOURCES

INTRODUCTION

In a world where many search for purpose, guidance, and spiritual fulfilment, Jesus Christ stands as a timeless and universal figure. This manuscript serves as a humble guide, inviting us to embark on a profound journey of encountering, experiencing, and truly understanding Jesus—a pilgrimage that has the potential to reshape our very existence. Will you join this journey with unwavering dedication, placing Christ at the core of every aspect of your life?

Psalm 147 reminds us that you are a manifestation of God's thoughts. Even before your conception, you existed in the depths of God's heart. You were envisioned, carefully crafted, and deeply cherished by Him. You are not a mere coincidence; you are a deliberate creation. The Creator intricately designed you, recorded His intentions in His book, and brought you into existence. As His masterpiece, you possess immeasurable value.

As you immerse yourself in the revelation of God's heart, you will be profoundly moved, experience healing, freedom, and transformation. Step by step, you will discover the path to genuine love and the life-changing grace it brings.

Bible Verses

- "For God so loved the world that he gave his one and only Son, that whoever believes in him shall not perish but have eternal life." - John 3:16
- "I am the way, the truth, and the life. No one comes to the Father except through me." - John 14:6
- "I have come that they may have life, and have it to the full." - John 10:10)

A Prayer to Begin Our Journey

Dear Heavenly Father, I believe that You see, know, and love me deeply. You are my greatest advocate. As I begin this book, I seek Your guidance to see myself as You do and to understand Your divine nature. Grant me a pure vision of You, and deepen my knowledge of Your presence. Help me foster a closer bond with You and be a better friend to You.

I dedicate myself to this pursuit, knowing that even small steps please Your heart. I declare my unwavering "yes" to Your call, leaving behind fear and mediocrity. I long for wholeness and for all Your blessings of righteousness, peace, and joy.

I surrender to Your divine will, asking You to mend, liberate, fill, and enable me to manifest Your dream for my life. I offer these requests in Jesus' name and express my gratitude in advance. Amen.

Today, as you step forward, embrace a newfound freedom rooted in the revelation of God's unconditional love!

1

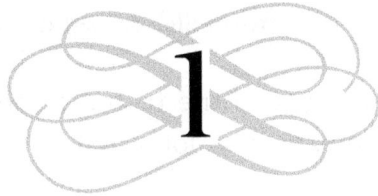

Exploring the Quest for Truth

In our vast world, an inner restlessness and deep longing reside within human hearts. From towering mountains to deep valleys, across oceans and lands, a universal thread weaves through our lives—a hunger for truth and an unyielding pursuit of fulfilment.

Many embark on this noble journey, seeking meaning through diverse paths. Some explore the depths of philosophy and science, hoping to unravel the mysteries of the universe. Others amass possessions and wealth, seeking to fill their inner void with earthly treasures. Still, some yearn for significance in relationships, longing for love and acceptance to banish the void.

Despite our technological advances, an unquenched thirst for truth persists. The pursuit of wealth often leaves hearts hollow and unsatisfied. Even amid loving relationships, a lingering emptiness endures—an insatiable hunger unmet by human connections alone.

In the midst of this tireless quest, a figure emerges—Jesus Christ, truth in human form, the very essence of fulfilment. Beyond a philosopher or teacher, He is the ultimate source of life's deepest desires. In the Scriptures,

"I am the life, the way, and the truth. No one else but Me is the only way to the Father" - John 14:6

He isn't merely a guide; he is the exclusive path to truth and fulfilment. All other roads lead to disappointment.

In Jesus, we discover the essence of truth, embodying divine wisdom as the rhema word, revealing the heart of God in a world shrouded in confusion. His words cut through the darkness, illuminating the path to real life and purpose.

Moreover, Jesus claims to be the source of life—the eternal spring of true fulfilment. While the world offers fleeting pleasures, only in Christ do we find enduring contentment. He alone satisfies our deepest longings, granting a peace beyond comprehension.

As we embark on this journey, let's abandon the world's empty promises and fix our gaze on Jesus. In Him, we uncover a truth beyond grasp and experience fulfilment beyond imagination. May our hearts remain open, our minds ready as we embark on a pilgrimage to the One who is the way, the truth, and the life—the ultimate fulfilment of our deepest desires.

2

Embracing the Profound Message of Jesus

Isaiah 55:6 advises us to seek the Lord while He's near. Understanding the historical context of Jesus' life and teachings is crucial as we explore His person and legacy. It helps us grasp the immense significance of His words and actions. Jesus wasn't merely a wise teacher or charismatic leader; Jesus, God's Son, sent to reveal the Father's heart and redeem a broken world.

As we examine Jesus' life, we're deeply touched by the fundamental principles that defined His mission: love, compassion, forgiveness, and prioritising others. These weren't abstract concepts to Jesus; they manifested in every interaction. He loved the unlovable, showed kindness to the marginalised, forgave the seemingly unforgivable, and lived selflessly, inspiring and challenging us.

Among Jesus' teachings, His revolutionary concept of the kingdom stands out. He spoke of a kingdom that overturned worldly values—a realm where humility triumphed over pride, where the last were elevated to the first, and where the spiritually impoverished received heavenly wealth. This message defied societal norms then and continues to confront today's culture.

In a world often exalting power, personal success, and self-centeredness, Jesus' message of humility, servitude, and sacrificial love remains radical and demanding, urging us to align our lives with His teachings.

Jesus' message is profoundly transformative. Fully embracing Jesus' revolutionary message requires surrender and obedience, relinquishing our desires, taking up our cross daily, and following Him with unwavering devotion.

In a world often marred by conflict and selfishness, Jesus' teaching shines like a ray of hope, offering an alternative path leading to true fulfilment, joy, and peace.

May we diligently seek the Lord while He's near. Let's wholeheartedly absorb Jesus' profound message and let it transform us. May His love, compassion, forgiveness, and selflessness illuminate our lives, reflecting His kingdom here on earth.

"Seek the LORD while He may be found, Call upon Him while He is near." - Isaiah 55:6

3

Opening the Heart to Encounter

Open Your Heart to Encounter Jesus. To truly meet Jesus face-to-face, we must open our hearts wide. The state of our hearts significantly influences our ability to understand our Lord deeply. As we explore the journey of encountering Jesus, we must cultivate a heart that is open and ready to embrace the incredible wonders He has for us.

Prayer is the gateway to unlocking our hearts, allowing the Holy Spirit to work within us. Through prayer, we invite God to explore the deepest parts of our being, revealing our desires, fears, and uncertainties. This prepares us for an authentic encounter with Jesus.

Meditation and contemplation—these practices further enhance our connection with Jesus. By setting aside time to quiet our hearts and minds, we create a sacred space for God's voice to resonate within us. As we meditate on His Word and contemplate His character, our understanding deepens, and our encounters become more transformative. As Psalm 46:10 wisely says,

"Be still, and know that I am God."

In moments of tranquility and silence, we uncover the profound reality that God is present with us, fervently desiring to reveal Himself to those who seek Him

Now, let's explore the inspiring stories of individuals who, with open hearts, encountered Jesus in profound ways that changed their lives.

Sarah: When she poured her heart out to the Lord in prayer during a time of uncertainty and bewilderment about her mission, she had a profound encounter with Jesus. She was by herself in her room when she sensed Jesus' undeniable, palpable presence—a profound serenity that dispelled all doubt. His love enveloped her, granting her clarity of purpose and unwavering hope.

David: Burdened by guilt and shame, he found forgiveness and liberation when he confessed his sins to Jesus.

Mark: Weighed down by past regrets, he encountered the redeeming power of Jesus through intentional prayer and meditation on God's forgiveness and grace.

Matthew (Levi): A tax collector, he left everything to follow Jesus, experiencing a complete transformation. His story illustrates the transformative potency of Christ's call, reminding us that no one is beyond the reach of God's love and grace.

These testimonies remind us that encountering Jesus is not abstract; it's a tangible reality. By engaging in prayer, reflection, and contemplation, we open up a channel for Jesus to speak to us and alter us from the inside out.

Fostering our connection with Jesus involves delving into the living Word of God. The Bible isn't merely a collection of age-old wisdom; it's vibrant and alive. The Holy Spirit makes God's heart known to us when we read and meditate on Scripture, which helps us understand God's truths and character more deeply and insightfully. God's words have the POWER to change our lives.

Revelation 3:20 as we proceed on our journey:

"Look, I am standing at the door and knocking. I will enter if someone hears my voice and opens the door."

Keep an open mind and heart, because you can only find true fulfilment, meaning, and eternal joy in His presence.

4

Walking in Relationship with Jesus/Cultivating an Intimate Relationship with Jesus

Greetings, as we embark on this journey of walking closely with Jesus, it's crucial to grasp the profound importance of cultivating a personal and intimate bond with our Saviour. It's always not enough to know about Jesus existence. It is His desire for us to have a profound and genuine connection with Him, a connection that changes us and brings us closer to the essence of our Heavenly Father.

Amidst the busyness of our daily lives, it can be easy to overlook what genuinely holds significance. We might get caught up in religious routines or debates, forgetting that Jesus seeks more than just our head knowledge or rituals. He yearns for our hearts—our genuine, undivided love and devotion.

To develop this connection, we must first understand the roles of faith, trust, and surrender. Faith lays the groundwork for our relationship with

Jesus. We express our acceptance of Him as our Lord and Savior through faith, particularly in His work on the cross. However, faith isn't a single moment; it's a continuous voyage of confidence and dependence on Him.

Trusting Jesus involves handing over our plans, desires, and wills to Him. It means admitting that His ways are higher and His thoughts greater. Surrender demands humility and a willingness to let go of our understanding and control. It's an ongoing process of dying to ourselves and letting Jesus lead us.

Practicality is key in our walk with Jesus. We need to invite Him into every corner of our lives—our work, relationships, decisions, and even mundane routines. Jesus isn't distant, reserved for Sundays; He's our constant companion, ready to guide and transform if we let Him in.

A way to welcome Jesus into our lives is through prayer. It's not a one-way talk but an intimate dialogue with our Saviour. It's about sharing our joys, concerns, and needs with Him. It's also about listening and finding His guidance and presence in the quiet. Prayer aligns our hearts with His will and opens us up to His transformation.

Immersing ourselves in God's Word is vital for nurturing our relationship with Jesus. The Bible isn't just old wisdom; it's God's living Word. As we read and reflect, the Spirit unveils God's heart, showing His character and purpose. Through Scripture, we meet Jesus Himself—the Word in flesh. It's where we find nourishment, correction, and wisdom to walk righteously.

Finally, walking closely with Jesus involves active participation in the community of believers. We're not meant to journey alone; we need fellow followers of Christ. Gathering for worship, fellowship, and service strengthens our faith. In the community, we experience Christ's love tangibly and become instruments of His love and healing for a broken world.

Dear friends, let's not settle for a surface-level faith or a distant bond with Jesus. He wants more for us. He desires to walk alongside, guide, and shape us. Let's surrender, trust His unchanging love, and invite Him into every aspect of our lives. As we do, we'll find joy, peace, and fulfilment that come from walking closely with our Saviour, Jesus Christ.

5

Transformation Through Encounter: Unveiling Inner Healing, Liberation, and Purpose in Jesus

"Come to me, all who are weary and burdened, and I will give you rest." - Matthew 11:28

In the preceding chapters, we've delved into the life-altering impact of encountering Jesus. We've explored how such encounters usher in hope, peace, and joy that defy understanding. Now, let's venture deeper into the transformative heart of meeting Jesus, focusing on inner restoration, freedom, and a renewed sense of purpose.

As we navigate our faith journey, let's not underestimate the transformative potential of encountering Jesus. The mere presence of Jesus possesses the power to pierce our hearts, catalysing profound inner healing, liberating us from bondage, and rekindling a fresh purpose within. In this chapter, we'll explore the incredible ways Jesus encounters yield radical transformations that eternally change lives.

"Dear friends, let's fix our eyes on Jesus, the pioneer and perfecter of faith. For the joy set before him, he endured the cross, scorning its shame, and sat down at the right hand of the throne of God." - Hebrews 12:2

"He heals the brokenhearted and binds up their wounds." - Psalm 147:3

"Create in me a clean heart, O God, and renew a right spirit within me." - Psalm 51:10

Many of us carry within us scars, pain, and brokenness. Life may have dealt us wounds, disappointments, or traumas that left us shattered and in dire need of healing. But take heart; encountering Jesus carries the power to mend our shattered pieces.

When Jesus enters our encounter, His love and compassion penetrate deep into our souls. He ministers to our emotional injuries, catalysing forgiveness and enabling us to forgive those who've wounded us. As we surrender our brokenness to Him, He meticulously restores and fills our hearts.

In the role of the ultimate Healer, Jesus carefully tends to our wounded hearts. As we offer our pain to Him, He gently stitches our wounds and anoints them with His healing touch. In His presence, we discover comfort, solace, and the unwavering assurance that our past doesn't define us. His transformative touch births beauty from ashes and turns mourning into dancing.

A remarkable facet of encountering Jesus is how He brings healing to our deepest hurts, restoring our brokenness. Jesus' love holds the capacity to reach even the darkest corners of our being, exposing our pain and granting healing. Through these encounters, the blind regain sight, the oppressed find freedom, and the brokenhearted are made whole.

Remember Sarah's story? She once carried the weight of past errors, burdened by guilt and shame. Her progress was stifled by these heavy chains. Yet, when Sarah encountered Jesus, His forgiveness poured over her like a rushing stream. In His presence, she discovered a freedom previously foreign to her. His love shattered the chains that confined her, and she emerged transformed, bearing a renewed spirit and a restored identity.

"So if the Son sets you free, you will be free indeed." - John 8:36

Encountering Jesus isn't just about inner healing; it's about genuine liberation. Jesus came to break the shackles that bind us, freeing us from sin, guilt, shame, and the clutches of evil.

In His encounter, Jesus' truth releases us from the falsehoods that held us captive. His grace envelops our sins, empowering us to conquer victoriously. Unchained from fear and sin, we undergo transformation, becoming children of God, ready to embrace His love and purpose to the fullest.

Through His sacrificial cross, Jesus paid for our freedom. He conquered sin and death, ushering in new life. In His presence, we gain the power to overcome the strongholds that once ensnared us. We no longer yield to fear, guilt, or shame. Instead, we stand empowered to walk righteously, glorifying God with our lives.

Consider John's journey - a life ensnared by addiction. His existence spiralled out of control, and hope became a distant memory. Then, in a moment of surrender, John met Jesus. Through His love and grace, John escaped the clutches of addiction. His life metamorphosed into a living testament to the power of encountering Jesus. Today, John thrives in the freedom only Jesus imparts, igniting transformation through encounters with the Savior.

"For we are God's masterpiece. He has created us anew in Christ Jesus, so we can do the good things he planned for us long ago." - Ephesians 2:10

Encountering Jesus yields inner healing, freedom, and a revived purpose. In His presence, aimlessness dissipates, replaced by a grander perspective. We find ourselves woven into God's divine blueprint.

Jesus unveils His purpose for our lives, inviting us to join His redemptive work. He equips us with His Spirit and gifts, empowering us to make a difference in a fractured world. These encounters ignite a passion to serve, share love, and mend the world's brokenness.

Mark's story encapsulates this truth. Once a seeker of worldly success and material wealth, Mark encountered Jesus, forever altering his course. The veil of illusion lifted, exposing the emptiness of his pursuits. Jesus revealed to him a divine purpose grounded in service, hope, and the transformative might of meeting Him. Changing Mark's life forever, he embraced the calling of Jesus.

"Anyone who belongs to Christ has become a new person. The old life is gone; a new life has begun!" - 2 Corinthians 5:17

Lives have been changed following the encounter with Jesus. The fact that the disciples abandoned their earthly lives to follow Jesus, especially the conversion of Paul's during the Road to Damascus

Testimonies abound – addicts set free, broken hearts restored, and the lost finding their way. Jesus has turned anger into love, greed into generosity, and pride into humility. These stories underscore the reach of Jesus' transformative love.

Even today, we witness lives being transformed. Addicts emerge from the abyss, relationships mend, and despair is replaced with joy. These stories remind us that encountering Jesus transcends religiosity, engendering profound change.

My dearest readers, never underestimate Jesus' power in your life. He transforms, heals, and liberates. As we open our hearts, entrusting ourselves to Him, we become His, forever changed. Seek His presence and be transformed into vessels of His love, grace, and truth. In encountering Jesus, life flourishes, purpose ignites, and God is glorified.

6

Spreading the Experience: Igniting Transformation

As outlined in Matthew 28:19–20, we are called to both personally encounter and share the limitless love and grace of our Lord Jesus Christ. Our deep relationship with Jesus is not just a privilege but also a duty, urging us to propagate His name globally. Sharing our personal encounters with Jesus is not about self-promotion; it's a means of testifying to the life-changing power of His love, echoing Paul's message in Romans 10:13–14. Through our personal accounts, others may find the path to establishing a profound connection with Jesus as they witness the transformative impact of God's work in our lives.

Moreover, sharing encounters should not be reserved for special occasions but should flow naturally from hearts brimming with love for Him and a desire for others to know His salvation. We should seize every opportunity to speak of His goodness and grace, whether to family, friends, colleagues, or strangers.

Approach these conversations with gentleness and respect; we should seek to understand before being understood. Grace and love should season our words, reflecting Christ's character, as encouraged in the following verse

"But sanctify the Lord God in your hearts, and always *be* ready to *give* a defense to everyone who asks you a reason for the hope that is in you, with meekness and fear." 1 Peter 3:15

However, sharing encounters is not solely an individual task. Community and accountability are crucial in our relationship with Jesus and in spreading His message. To create a supportive Christian community, as stated :

"And let us consider one another in order to stir up love and good works, not forsaking the assembling of ourselves together, as *is* the manner of some, but exhorting *one another,* and so much more as you see the Day approaching." Hebrews 10:24-25

The passage provides strength and inspiration to live life according to Jesus' teachings. In a world often hostile to truth, fellowship becomes an oasis of encouragement that equips us to boldly share our faith.

Living out Jesus' teachings and impacting the world go hand in hand with sharing encounters. It's not enough to merely talk about faith; our lives must tangibly reflect Jesus. The world should see His love, compassion, and selflessness in us, not just hear about Him. We must demonstrate His transformative power through both our words and actions.

We have been entrusted with the Gospel's good news, and it is our duty to proclaim it boldly through our lives. By showing His love through kindness, service, and sacrificial love, we unveil the Gospel's transformative power to the world.

Therefore, dear brothers and sisters, let us be fervent in sharing encounters. Let's not grow weary or complacent in our mission to disciple all nations. The Great Commission is not a mere suggestion; it's a divine command. Equipped by the Holy Spirit, let's bear witness to the life-changing power of Jesus Christ. May our encounters transform the world as we faithfully share them.

"And he said to them, 'Go into all the world and proclaim the gospel to the whole creation.'" - Mark 16:15

7

Encountering God in the Midst of Trials: A Spiritual Journey of Transformation

In the depths of the night, the patriarch Jacob embarked on a journey that transcended the physical realm. With his two wives, servants, and eleven sons safely across the ford of Jabbok, he stood alone spiritually, poised at the threshold of an extraordinary encounter. It was not just a wrestling match with a mysterious man, but a profound spiritual struggle that would unveil the very core of Jacob's being – a struggle borne from his longing for divine blessing.

Through the night's quiet hours, Jacob grappled with the enigmatic angelic figure, resolute in his determination to secure a blessing. This gruelling contest embodied not only his physical tenacity but also his unyielding spirit to engage with God. Dawn approached, and in a moment of sheer determination, the man struck Jacob's hip, leaving him with a lasting limp. Still, Jacob clung to his divine opponent, vowing, "I will not let you go unless you bless me."

The man's response marked a turning point in Jacob's life. Bestowing upon him the name Israel, meaning "he struggles with God," this encounter brought about a transformation. His victory was not through physical prowess but through surrendering his will to God's.

Peniel, the place of encounter, took on a new meaning for Jacob. Here, he had beheld the face of God and survived. A man who was once manipulative and deceitful now bore the mark of this divine encounter, displaying God's supremacy.

In our journey, we will encounter trials and temptations that leave us vulnerable. Yet, we can draw strength from Jacob's experience. He did not recoil from the struggle; rather, he clung tighter, unwavering in his pursuit of God's blessing.

The book of Job echoes this sentiment, which vividly portrays Job's acquaintance with suffering. Job's agonising quest for understanding and justice led him to question the very foundation of his faith. In response, God revealed Himself in the midst of his uncertainty, gently reminding Job of His boundless wisdom and authority.

Job's humility in the face of the Divine's grandeur paved the way for restoration and renewed faith. He surrendered his finite comprehension to the infinite wisdom of God, emerging from the ordeal with a profound grasp of God's sovereign ways.

In our moments of wrestling with God, let us learn wisdom from Jacob and Job alike. By embracing the struggle, persistently seeking God's favour, and submitting to His wisdom, we bring forth transformation in ourselves.

Though the scars of our trials stay with us, marked and limping, they also bear the promise of divine blessing and growth.

Though our journey through life may be filled with trials and tribulations, let us remember that encounters with God in the midst of our struggles are invitations for change. Just as Jacob and Job emerged from their trials, we too can emerge victorious. The struggle is not in vain; it is a catalyst for our spiritual transformation.

8

Worship God in total surrendering: A Journey Beyond Entertainment

In 2 Samuel 6:12-23, we witness how the act of surrender and worship leads to a profound encounter with God. David's narrative unfolds as we see him dancing before the Lord with both joy and reverence during the procession of the ark throughout the city. This was no ordinary dance; it was a dance of unreserved surrender.

As each step of the ark resonated, David paused to offer sacrifices—a bull and a fattened calf. Cloaked in a simple linen ephod, his heart's devotion was unwavering, his worship extravagant. The resounding shouts and trumpet blasts underscored the jubilant atmosphere as Israel embraced the presence of the Almighty.

In the midst of this fervour, Michal, Saul's daughter, cast a disdainful glance at David's exuberance. Contempt for his unabashed worship welled up in her heart. Yet David's response reverberates with timeless wisdom. He declared, "I will celebrate before the LORD. I will become even more undignified than this." David recognized that authentic worship transcends human opinions and that humility before God is the pinnacle of honour.

Acts 16:16-34 unveils another form of encountering God through worship amid adversity. Paul and Silas, battered and confined, burst into prayer and hymns. The melodies of surrender echoed within their chains as their spirits soared despite the dire circumstances. The ensuing earthquake, which broke their chains, demonstrates worship's transformative power in the face of suffering.

David's dance and Paul and Silas' hymns collectively illuminate worship as a posture of surrender—a channel to open ourselves entirely to God's presence. Within the act of worship, we cast aside self-consciousness, pride, and societal judgments. We echo David's resolve, embracing the undignified path that leads to divine honour.

The power of worship is not limited by a specific location, time, or scenario—it permeates every facet of life. By relinquishing control and embracing vulnerability and humility, we invite God's transformative power into our lives. The dance of David and the hymns of Paul and Silas epitomise that worship is both a response to God's majesty and an agent of profound change.

May we, akin to them, bear living witness to worship's strength amidst trials. In spite of burdens weighing heavy, may our hearts lift melodies of surrender to the heavens. As we sway and sing in devotion, may God's presence resonate, shattering chains and setting captives free. Let's engrave within ourselves the understanding that authentic worship, firmly entwined with genuine surrender, beckons God's transformative touch into our lives and into the lives of those around us.

Thus, with the courage of David and the faith of Paul and Silas, let us embrace both the power and act of surrender and worship. Through the cadence of our lives, let us compose a symphony that welcomes God's presence to reshape us and our circumstances. In the pursuit of encountering God, may our worship serve as the canvas on which the masterpiece of His transformation unfolds—a journey that leads us toward the divine, our Heavenly Father!

9

God's Faithfulness in the Wilderness

The passages of Exodus 19-20 reveal a defining moment for the Israelites as they journeyed through the wilderness. God's unwavering faithfulness guided them to the sacred ground of Mount Sinai, where His presence manifested in profound ways. Through this encounter, God not only recounted His deliverance from Egypt but also showcased His might and compassion. In awe of His holiness, the Israelites witnessed His sovereignty and entered into a covenant relationship with Him.

In this pivotal interaction, God bestowed the Ten Commandments upon the Israelites. These commandments were not meant to confine but to provide a framework for righteous living, reflecting God's very nature. Rooted in His faithfulness, these laws were a testament to His desire for the Israelites to live harmoniously with Him and with each other. Through this encounter, God unveiled His heart's intent—to shape His chosen people into a holy nation, a kingdom of priests.

Similarly, Jesus' temptation in the wilderness, stated in Matthew 4:1-11, stands as a profound testament to His unwavering commitment to the

Father's will amidst temptation. After forty days of fasting, Jesus confronted Satan, who aimed to divert Him from His divine mission. Temptations appealing to Jesus' physical needs, quest for power, and yearning for recognition were presented. Yet Jesus stood firm, anchoring Himself in God's Word and the power of the Holy Spirit.

In the wilderness, Jesus displayed resolute trust in God's faithfulness. Earthly temptations were rejected in favour of honouring and obeying God. His confrontation with temptation underscored His steadfast dedication to fulfilling the Father's will, triumphing over the enemy's schemes.

Both the Israelites' encounter at Mount Sinai and Jesus' wilderness temptation unveil the tapestry of God's faithfulness and our corresponding response. God's aim is to forge a covenant relationship with His people, guiding them toward righteousness and holiness. Just as the Israelites embraced the call to honour the commandments and be set apart, we too are summoned to uphold God's directives and navigate life in alignment with Him.

Jesus' example underscores the value of anchoring ourselves in God's Word and the Holy Spirit's empowerment amid temptation. It reminds us that God's faithfulness remains steadfast during times of hardship. His strength empowers us to resist sin's temptations and remain steadfast in our commitment to His will. These encounters affirm God's enduring faithfulness across generations, never swaying from His promises.

Dear friends, may our encounters with God in the wilderness bolster our faith in His faithfulness. May we perceive them as emblems of His love and guidance. Let us cling to His commandments, illuminated by His Word, a guiding lamp for each step:

"Your word is a lamp unto my feet a light onto my path." - Psalm 119:105

In the wilderness seasons of life, may we draw near to God, certain that He journeys with us—faithfully leading and sustaining us through unwavering love:

"Trust in the Lord with all your heart and lean not on your own understanding, in all your ways submit to Him and He will make your paths straight." - Proverb 3:5-6

10

Healing Embrace of God:
Healing and Miracles

In the depths of our human brokenness, an innate yearning arises—an ache for the balm of healing and the wonder of miracles. We find ourselves reaching out, longing for the touch of God to restore our weary souls. It's in these moments that our Lord Jesus Christ responds, His boundless compassion and tenderness resonating in response to our heartfelt cries for help.

In this chapter, let us explore two profound encounters between Jesus and those who were desperate for His healing touch. These encounters will reveal the power of haith and the miracles of our Saviour.

Our first journey transports us to Matthew 9:1-8 and is mentioned in Mark 2:1-12; a modest abode in Capernaum, where Jesus held court before a gathering. Amid the eager crowd was a man paralysed, carried by four friends who harboured a steadfast resolve to present their companion into the very presence of the Healer.

Upon approaching the house where Jesus spoke, it was crowded with onlookers. However, the four men, in the face of discouragement, refused to submit to any obstacles. In a display of resourceful determination, they carried their paralysed friend onto the roof, dismantled it, and lowered him into the very presence of Jesus.

Can you feel the gravity of the scene? The paralytic lay there before Jesus, his companions peering down with hope suspended in the air. Jesus, in His gaze, perceived not only the paralysis that gripped the man's limbs but the intricate layers of spiritual and emotional anguish that bound his heart.

And in that poignant instant, Jesus uttered words that reverberate through time, "Son, your sins are forgiven." The tenderness that laced His voice touched the very soul of the paralytic, reaching the core of his being. Beyond the shackles of physical ailment, Jesus discerned a far deeper yearning—the need for reconciliation with God.

Yet, amidst this sacred exchange, religious leaders in attendance hastened to judge and challenge Jesus' authority to grant forgiveness. However, Jesus, in His divine wisdom, responded to their challenge. Jesus responded : "Which is easier to say: 'Your sins are forgiven,' or 'Rise, take up your bed and walk'?"

To emphasise His authority and the power that surged within Him, Jesus turned to the paralytic and proclaimed, "I say to you, rise, pick up your bed, and go home." In an instant, newfound strength coursed through the man's limbs, carrying him to his feet. He arose, carrying the very bed that had once imprisoned him. The crowd stood witness to a miracle that surpassed their wildest expectations.

This encounter unravels a tapestry woven with the threads of faith, forgiveness, and physical restoration. The four men displayed unwavering faith in the face of adversity, overcoming any obstacle that would prevent them from being in the presence of Jesus. And in response, Jesus pours forth compassion, fulfilling man's spiritual and physical needs in a single, majestic sweep.

As we now turn our focus to the story of Lazarus in John 11, we witness Jesus' mastery over death itself. In the village of Bethany, which Jesus and His disciples had visited multiple times before, Lazarus, a dear friend, succumbed to illness. Lazarus' sisters, Martha and Mary, sent a message to Jesus, pleading to Him with desperation. Despite their plea, Jesus purposefully waited for two days upon receiving their message. Although this confused both Martha and Mary, the delay was a singular brushstroke on a larger canvas, one that was to unveil His glory and bountiful love.

Upon Jesus' arrival in Bethany, Lazarus had already rested within the tomb for four days. Filled with grief, Martha ventured to meet Jesus. Amidst her sorrow, she tenderly expressed her faith, affirming,

"Lord, if you had been here, my brother wouldn't have died. Yet even now I know that whatever you ask from God, God will give you."

Although Martha may have experienced anguish over His delay, her overwhelming faith in Him was evident. She believed in Jesus' potential to bring healing and restoration, even when overshadowed by the spectre of death. And in response, Jesus, moved by her faith and gently brushed by her sorrow, declared,

"I am the resurrection and the life. Whoever believes in me, though he die, yet shall he live." - John 11:25,26

The stage then shifts, casting light upon Lazarus' tomb. Here, Jesus, moved by the swirl of grief that enveloped Him, shed tears alongside those who mourned. With a command that echoes through time, He bellowed, "Lazarus, come out!" In this transcendent moment, the potency of life triumphed over the grip of death as Lazarus emerged, freed from the suffocating cocoon of grave clothes.

The resurrection of Lazarus speaks to a profound truth—Jesus is not only the giver of life but also the conqueror of death itself. He beckons us to anchor our faith in Him, even amidst the abyss of our deepest pain and loss. We're invited to grasp the truth that He wields the authority to usher in resurrection and life.

Dear brothers and sisters, as we stand in contemplation of these encounters between Jesus and those who hungered for healing, let us approach God with the humility of a heart aflame with faith. In this reflection, let's be mindful of His boundless compassion and gentleness, recognizing that He gazes upon our brokenness and stands ready to meet us precisely where we are.

As we ardently seek to encounter the healing touch and miracles of God, let us mirror the resolve of the paralytic's friends—persistent, unwavering, and fervently rooted in faith. Amidst the shadows of sorrow and loss, let's seek refuge in the words of Martha, a declaration that echoes through time, confirming our faith in Jesus as the resurrection and the life.

May the surge of God's healing touch and the vibrant reality of His miraculous works continue to shape and transfigure our lives, birthing forth a testimony that radiates His glory and compassion. Let's approach Him with hearts wide open, ready to encounter the profound, life-altering love of our Saviour.

11

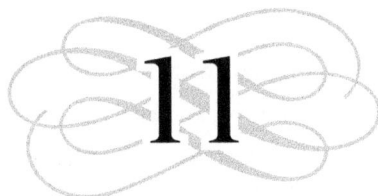

The Overflow of God's Provision and Abundance

In the Bible, we can find a story of Jesus addressing a large congregation who wish to seek both spiritual and physical nourishment, as told in Matthew 14:13-21. This event illuminates God's miraculous provision, echoing the promise in:

"And my God will meet all your needs according to the riches of His glory in Christ Jesus." - Philippians 4:19

Out in the wilderness, this congregation gathered, drawn by Jesus' teachings and His captivating presence. Their hunger was not solely for His teachings but also for spiritual fufilment. The twelve disciples started to turn the crowd away, as the crowd was hungry and they could not feed them. Then Jesus, their compassionate Saviour, uttered words that challenged His disciples:

"They need not go away; you give them something to eat" -
Matthew 14:16

Caught off guard, the disciples' disbelief stemmed from their limited resources—only five loaves of bread and two fish. However, Jesus, the Great Provider, transcends human constraints. In His hands, meagre offerings cascaded into torrents of abundance. He raised the loaves and fish heavenward, invoking blessings, and distributed what was offered. Astonishingly, all were satisfied, with twelve baskets of left overs.

This miracle testifies to God's boundless provision, transforming our insufficiencies into extravagant plenty. In our lives, when resources seem scarce, we must remember that our God is a God of lavish abundance.

Now, let's journey to 1 Kings 17:8-16, where a drought plagued the land in Elijah's time. A widow in Zarephath stood at the intersection of scarcity and despair, possessing only a handful of flour and a little oil.

Elijah's humble request for sustenance challenged her grim circumstances. His words kindled hope:

"Do not fear; go and do as you have said. But first, make me a little cake of it and bring it to me, and afterward, make something for yourself and your son." - 1 Kings 17:13

Though these instructions defied reason, the widow's faith surpassed logic. By faith, she obeyed the prophet's words. Remarkably, the jar of flour and the oil became fountains of unending sustenance until the rain quenched the land's thirst.

In this encounter, we witness God's faithfulness and provision amid scarcity. The widow's surrender of her meagre offering unlocked divine abundance. Her obedience paved the way for supernatural intervention.

Today, we may face scarcity in various aspects of life—financial, emotional, or physical resources. Yet, let us not despair, for our unchanging God delights in providing for His children, even in the shadows of lack. Our obedience and surrender open the door to His miraculous provision.

As we reflect on these encounters, let our faith ignite. Approach the Heavenly Father with unwavering confidence, knowing that He can provide even when the table seems bare. Our God embodies abundance, and His provision transcends limitations. Trust Him, lean into His presence, and witness His miraculous provision unfold in every facet of your life.

12

The Heart of God: Justice and Compassion Unveiled

Beloved friends, as we venture deeper into the tapestry of God's Word, let the doors of our hearts fling wide open to the echoes of His justice and the tender embrace of His compassion. Our Saviour, Jesus Christ, etched these divine attributes into the very fabric of His earthly ministry. Let us now observe two other encounters that show God's heart for justice as well as His unyielding welspring of compassion.

The Good Samaritan, Luke 10:25-37;   In Luke's Gospel, we are told of a dialogue between Jesus and a lawyer, a seeker of truth who aimed to test the depth of the teacher's wisdom. With earnest inquiry, the lawyer inquired, "Teacher, what shall I do to inherit eternal life?" Jesus, who is a source of boundless wisdom, answered with two pillars of the commandments—to love God with all its entirety and to love neighbours as one loves oneself.

Yet the lawyer, driven by a desire to vindicate himself, probed further:

"And who is my neighbour?" And thus, Jesus unfurled the tale of the Good Samaritan—a story that demolished cultural division and demonstrated what it means to have genuine compassion. This parable whispers of a traveller, beaten and left half-dead along the wayside. A priest and a Levite, the vanguards of religious rigour, passed by, avoiding the traveler without a drop of compassion. Yet a Samaritan—who historically were scorned by Israelites—marched forth and had mercy upon the traveler's suffering and misfortune. He bound the wounded and carried him, and the Samaritan nursed the traveler to health

Upon concluding the story, Jesus questioned the lawyer, "Which of these three, do you think, proved to be a neighbour to the man who fell among the robbers?" The lawyer, compelled by the parable's truth, answered, "The one who showed him mercy." To this, Jesus replied, "You go, and do likewise."

The Good Samaritan beckons us beyond the confines of culture, ethnicity, and class. It is an invitation to live a life of compassion without prejudice. It beseeches us to be conduits of justice and advocates for the downtrodden. May we be reminded of this call as we mirror the heart of our Saviour.

As we turn our gaze to another tale, The Woman with the Issue of Blood, Luke 8:43-48; a passage adorned with threads of faith, healing, and compassion A woman's twelve-year torment, a ceaseless haemorrhage, left her depleted emotionally and hopeless. The corridors of the medical halls offered no solace. Yet, a spark of faith ignited within her—believing that even a touch of Jesus' garment could kindle the fire of her healing.

In the midst of a bustling crowd, this woman pushed through. She pressed through to graze the edge of Jesus' robe. In an instant, her ailment succumbed to His power, and her bleeding ceased. A ripple of recognition flowed from Him, and He asked, "Who touched me?" With trembling reverence, the woman bowed before Him, sharing her act and her story.

Jesus replied with compassion and tenderness: "Daughter, your faith has made you well; go in peace." In that sacred moment, Jesus not only sowed the seeds of physical healing but also bestowed upon her the crown of restored dignity—a cherished daughter of the Almighty.

This encounter ripples with the heart of Jesus, eternally ready to extend His healing touch to those cast aside by society. It is a poignant lesson that He peers beyond the masks we wear, addressing our deepest yearnings. Jesus yearns to restore not only our physical health but also our spiritual connection to Him in our lives.

As pilgrims of Christ, brothers and sisters, these encounters etch their wisdom in our souls. We are called to be catalysts of compassion for those on society's fringes. Let us, like Jesus, be instruments of justice and fountains of compassion. May our lives echo His love—bringing healing, renewal, and hope to a world ensnared by brokenness.

In quiet prayer, let our voices rise, "Heavenly Father, unshackle our sight to perceive the needs unfurling around us. Strengthen our hearts to be vessels of compassion and agents of justice. Teach us to love as You love—to embrace the broken, heal the hurting, and uplift the marginalised. Let the tapestry of our lives mirror Your mercy and grace. In the name of Jesus, we pray. Amen."

13

God's Wisdom and Revelation

Dear beloved brothers and sisters in Christ, today we embark on a transformative journey, exploring various encounters that shine light on God's wisdom and revelation in the lives of His people. Within the sacred Scriptures, two remarkable stories stand as living testaments to the power of encountering the divine. Let us now allow the word of God to enter our hearts to guide our own journeys.

Our first encounter leads us to the wise King Solomon. Recorded in 1 Kings 3:5-14, Solomon's dream came to fruition before us—a dream where the Almighty Himself extended a remarkable invitation:

"Ask for whatever you want me to give you." - 1 Kings 3:5

Such an extraordinary proposition! Solomon, acutely aware of his limitations and the gravity of his responsibilities, responded with a humble heart and a great desire to honour God.

Solomon's plea resonated with depth—he petitioned for wisdom to govern God's people righteously and to decipher between right and wrong, as shown in

"Therefore, give to Your servant an understanding heart to judge Your people, that I may discern between good and evil. For who is able to judge this great people of Yours?" - 1 Kings 3:9

What a profound request! It unveiled a heart yearning to lead with justice, serving the Lord faithfully. This plea found favour in the eyes of the Lord, for it mirrored a heart aligned with God's purposes. Not only did God bestow upon Solomon the wisdom he sought, but He also lavished him with wealth, honour, and a long life, as mentioned in 1 Kings 3:10-14.

This encounter between Solomon and God resounds with the significance of seeking and cherishing divine wisdom. Solomon's wisdom reverberated across nations, drawing kings and queens from distant realms to learn from his insights. His reign became a living testament to the power of encountering God and embracing His divine wisdom.

Now, let us shift our gaze to the second encounter—the meeting of the Ethiopian eunuch and Philip. Let us transport ourselves to Acts 8:26-39, where we encounter a devout traveler who had journeyed to Jerusalem for worship. On his return, this eunuch found himself engrossed in the scroll of Isaiah, yearning for wisdom. Guided by the Holy Spirit, Philip approached the eunuch's chariot.

Philip, responding to the Spirit's leading, began to share the Scriptures before the eunuch, delving into the prophetic words of Isaiah concerning

Jesus in Acts 8:32-35. Through divine revelation, the eunuch's understanding was ignited.

He acknowledged Jesus as the world's Saviour and the long-awaited Messiah. He begged for baptism with a heart aflame with faith, and Philip baptised him as a sign of his new status among the believers, found in Acts 8:36–38.

This encounter underscores the irreplaceable role of divine revelation in comprehending the complexity of the Scripture. Through the Holy Spirit's guidance and Philip's teaching, the eunuch's eyes were unveiled to the truth within God's Word. It magnifies the transformation borne of encountering God's wisdom and revelation—an encounter that births spiritual insight and fervent faith.

As we ponder these encounters, let us not stand idly by; instead, let us become active participants. Let us hunger for God's wisdom, mirroring the fervour of Solomon. May our hearts resound with attunement to His voice, seeking His guidance in every facet of life. As we approach the Scripture, may we do so with reverence, acknowledging that it is through divine revelation that our understanding is illuminated.

Dear friends, let us imitate the humility of Solomon, acknowledging our need for God's wisdom. Let us echo the eunuch's quest for understanding and recognise that it's through the teaching of God's Word that we encounter revelation. May we resist a surface-level grasp of Scripture and plunge into its depths, allowing God's wisdom and revelation to change our hearts and minds.

May the stories of Solomon and the Ethiopian eunuch radiate as guiding lights, illuminating our journey to seek God's wisdom and revelation. Through encountering Him, we unearth true comprehension, guidance, and the transformative energy that sets our lives ablaze.

May the Lord bless you abundantly as you pursue His wisdom and revelation within your unique faith voyage. Amen.

14

In God's Promises and Hope

In this chapter, we delve into two profound scriptural encounters that illuminate the enduring nature of God's promises and the radiant hope they instil. Our journey begins with the story of Abraham and the promise of descendants, found in Genesis 15:1-6. We then travel to the remarkable event on the road to Emmaus, where Jesus reveals His resurrection victory overcomes sin and death to the disciples, rekindling the flames of hope within them can be found in Luke 24:13-35.

Abraham and the Promise of Descendants

Abraham's life stands as a living testament to God's unwavering faithfulness in fulfilling His promises. Despite facing trials and obstacles, Abraham clung tenaciously to the promises God had bestowed on his life. Abraham and God have a touching conversation in Genesis 15:1-6, during which God confirms their commitment and promises to multiply Abraham's offspring as the stars in the sky.

This encounter symbolises the fundamental reality that we can cling to God's unwavering fidelity even in the midst of hardships. Abraham's steadfast faith, despite his advanced age and Sarah's barrenness, serves as an exemplary beacon for us. His unshakable trust in God's promise sets the stage for our own journey of faith.

Abraham's story encourages us to understand that God's promises transcend circumstances and human limitations. They are rooted in His unswerving faithfulness and boundless power. Abraham's resolute faith teaches us that, even when the realisation of God's promises seems distant, we can walk in faith, trusting in His perfect timing.

The Encounter on the Road to Emmaus

The encounter between Jesus and the disheartened disciples on the Emmaus road unfolds as a story of divine love, redemption, and the radiant hope that springs from Christ's resurrection. The aftermath of Jesus' crucifixion left the disciples in a cloud of despair. Their hope was eclipsed, unaware of the astonishing event that had occurred—the resurrection of their beloved Redeemer.

As they journeyed to Emmaus, Jesus joined them incognito. Through conversation, He unveiled the Scriptures, revealing the grand tapestry of God's plan. In the breaking of bread, their eyes were opened to the risen Christ in their midst, igniting a flame of hope in their hearts.

This encounter demonstrates the rhythm of God's faithfulness to His promises. It resonates as a symphony that echoes even in the depths of despair and uncertainty. It proclaims that, in moments of confusion, Jesus walks beside us, bearing the torch of hope. His resurrection victory overcomes sin and death, offering us the supreme hope—the hope of eternal life and reconciliation with the Divine.

Just as Jesus revealed Himself to the Emmaus-bound disciples, He continues to unveil His presence to us today. When we encounter the resurrected Christ, our hearts undergo transformation, and our hope finds its anchor. This encounter reinforces that, despite life's tumultuous trials, our God reigns victorious, and in Him, we discover an unshakeable hope.

As we navigate the stories of Abraham and the Emmaus travelers, we bear witness to the resilience of God's promises and the radiant hope they bring. Like Abraham, we are called to nurture unwavering faith, entrusting God to fulfil His promises in the face of challenges. The Emmaus encounter reminds us that Jesus is the source of our hope, with His resurrection illuminating our path to eternity.

On our individual faith journeys, may we firmly grasp the anchor of God's promises, drawing sustenance from His unwavering love and faithfulness. Let us find solace in the examples of Abraham and the Emmaus disciples— beacons who clung to God's promises and basked in His transformative power amid adversity. In God, we discover the fulfilment of all promises and the ultimate source of radiant hope for our lives.

15

God's Grace and Redemption

Within this chapter, let us set forth on a profound exploration of two moving encounters that illuminate the depths of God's grace and redemption. Through the lens of Luke 19:1-10's meeting between Jesus and Zacchaeus and the narrative of John 8:1-11 which captures Jesus' encounter with the adulterous woman, we unveil the transformative power of encountering Jesus and embracing His boundless grace.

Luke 19:1-10 brings us face-to-face with Zacchaeus, a tax collector alienated by society due to his corrupt dealings and allegiance to Roman authorities. Yet, beyond his flaws, Zacchaeus held a yearning to meet Jesus. Ascending a sycamore tree, he positioned himself to catch a mere glimpse of the passing Savior.

In a display of divine grace, Jesus recognized the earnest longing within Zacchaeus' heart.

"Zacchaeus, come down immediately. I must stay at your house today." - Luke 19:5

This was no happenstance; it was a divine appointment, woven by the threads of grace. Zacchaeus' response was nothing short of remarkable. Overflowing with joy and repentance, he declared,

"Behold, Lord, the half of my goods I give to the poor. And if I have defrauded anyone of anything, I restore it fourfold." - Luke 19:8

Zacchaeus was transformed by his meeting with Jesus and was inspired to make restitution and conform his life to God's will.

Zacchaeus' story underscores a timeless truth: God's grace and redemption extend to every corner of existence. No one is beyond the reach of His love. Jesus came as the seeker of the lost, and Zacchaeus' encounter highlights the boundless dimensions of His forgiveness.

John 8:1-11 unfolds another illustration of God's grace and redemption, The Woman Caught in Adultery. The religious authorities dragged before Jesus a woman ensnared in adultery, seeking to challenge Him in the legalistic web of Moses' law.

Jesus, the embodiment of wisdom and empathy, responded,

"If any one of you is without sin, let him be the first to throw a stone at her." - John 8:7

One by one, the accusers dispersed, their own imperfections laid bare.

Alone with the woman, Jesus asked,

"Woman, where are they? Has no one condemned you?" Her response was, "No one, sir." In that moment, Jesus pronounced, "Then neither do I condemn you. Go now and leave your life of sin." John 8:10-11

This encounter epitomises Jesus' grace to forgive and ability to provide us with a fresh beginning.

The adulterous woman, wrapped in Jesus' mercy, was shocked. Instead of condemnation, she received absolution and the beckoning to commence anew. This encounter vividly demonstrates encountering Jesus' grace, offering the transformative gift of redemption and a life redirected toward God's design.

Dear friends, in this chapter, we've embarked on a voyage through two compelling encounters—a duo that places God's grace and redemption in the spotlight. The rendezvous between Jesus and Zacchaeus charts a course of transformation, as a tax collector is bathed in the waters of forgiveness and love. The story of the adulterous woman illustrates the depth of Jesus' grace in a similar way, paving the way from judgement to restoration.

These true stories are interwoven into the very fabric of human existence and show the infinite reach of God's grace. They beckon us to approach Jesus with open hearts, for His grace is a transformative force that breaches every divide and His redemption is the compass leading us back to wholeness. In them, we find not mere anecdotes but living portraits of God's limitless love and our journey towards renewal.

16

God in the community and fellowship

In this chapter on encountering God through community and fellowship, it speaks of a powerful and transformative experience. Let's look at Acts 2:42-47 to unveil the early church's wholehearted embrace of this concept. With devotion to apostolic teachings, fellowship, the breaking of bread and prayer, they formed a unity that extended to caring for each other's needs. Through authentic love and selflessness, they bore witness to God's profound work among them.

In the same vein, Romans 1:8-15 narrates Paul's encounter with the believers in Rome. Beyond spiritual gifts, he yearned to visit them for mutual encouragement. This signifies the potential for reciprocal edification within a God-centred community—a testament to the potency of shared faith.

Wisdom, as Proverbs 4 illuminates, is a cornerstone of such communities. Pursuing comprehension and embracing divine truth fortifies bonds and nurtures unity. Wisdom steers us to harmonise traditions with timeless Scriptural truths, ensuring practices honour God and draw us nearer to Him.

"Wisdom is the principal thing; therefore, get wisdom. And in all your getting, get understanding." - Proverbs 4:7

Within communal nurturing, elevating children is pivotal. Jesus' words:

"Let the little children come to me" - Matthew 19:14

spotlight the importance of integrating and fostering young believers. By investing in their spiritual growth and cultivating a supportive environment, we pave their path to encountering God's love, grace, and truth.

Lastly, as we engage in community and fellowship, let God's supremacy prevail. Seeking His guidance, aligning with His will, and moulding our beliefs by His Word are our callings. Anchored in His truth, we forge an environment where encountering God becomes a tangible reality for each soul and the collective of believers.

May we persist in embracing the potency of community and fellowship in our pursuit of God's wisdom, the empowerment of children, the alignment of traditions with truth, and the relentless quest for His ultimate word. Through these practices, we shall encounter God in a profoundly transformative way—both individually and as a beloved collective.

17

The God in Times of Crisis and Suffering

Beloved brothers and sisters, today we delve into the depths of Scripture, exploring the encounters between faithful souls and the Almighty God amidst times of crisis and suffering. This chapter unveils two remarkable accounts: the saga of Shadrach, Meshach, and Abednego in the fiery furnace and Jesus' profound communion with God in the Garden of Gethsemane.

Let's take a look within the book of Daniel, which unfolds a powerful tale of three valiant Hebrew men thrust into a formidable trial—the fiery furnace. Shadrach, Meshach, and Abednego faced a life-altering choice: to bow before a golden idol or remain steadfast in their allegiance to the one true God.

Despite overwhelming pressure to conform, these devoted servants stood unwavering. They recognized that encountering God amidst suffering far outweighed earthly comforts. Their response echoes through time:

"If we are thrown into the blazing furnace, the God we serve is able to deliver us from it, and he will deliver us from Your Majesty's hand. But even if he does not, we want you to know, Your Majesty, that we will not serve your gods or worship the image of gold you have set up." - Daniel 3:17-18

In the searing blaze, a divine encounter unfolded. Rather than being consumed, Shadrach, Meshach, and Abednego beheld God's presence beside them. They emerged untouched, their faith fortified, and their testimony to God's might magnified.

We read about Jesus' intensely emotional experience with God in the Garden of Gethsemane in the book of Matthew. This moving scene occurs when Jesus finds refuge in the garden the night before he will be crucified and opens out to the Father. He sincerely begs,

"Oh Father, if it is possible, let this cup pass from me; nonetheless, not as I will, but as you will," - Matthew 26:39

knowing the anguish He will soon experience.

Amidst the garden's quiet, Jesus revealed complete surrender to the Father's plan, unmasking the depth of His love for humanity. Despite the weight of impending suffering and death, Jesus chose submission and obedience.

In this encounter, we grasp the essence of encountering God amid crisis. Jesus found peace, strength, and guidance in communion with the Father. His surrender, an offering of Himself, sets a model for believers—trusting in God's sovereignty even amid the harshest trials.

As we reflect upon the encounters between Shadrach, Meshach, and Abednego in the fiery furnace and Jesus in the Garden of Gethsemane, we confront unwavering faith and surrender to God's will that mark authentic encounters with Him during trials. These accounts urge us to seek His presence, trust His deliverance, and yield our lives wholly to His purpose.

Dear friends, may these tales of faith and encounter embolden us. In the fiercest fires and darkest valleys, remember—God is with us. He is our refuge, strength, and guide. Like Shadrach, Meshach, and Abednego, and like our Savior Jesus, may we encounter God amid trials, finding solace, courage, and steadfast faith in His presence.

May the grace and peace of our Lord Jesus Christ accompany you always.

18

Trials as Opportunities

Dear brothers and sisters, let's not underestimate the importance of trials, as James 1 reminds us:

"Consider it great joy, my brothers and sisters, whenever you experience trials of many kinds." - James 1:2

According to the Lord's teachings, these challenges provide valuable opportunities for personal growth and development. They act as catalysts for revealing our true potential and capabilities. Even when doubts and insecurities arise, God recognizes our abilities and intends for us to face trials, unveiling our resilience and the manageable nature of life's difficulties.

Avoiding our fears leads to a life filled with uncertainty and unease. However, when we confront our anxieties head-on and persevere through difficult times, we not only overcome personal obstacles but also gain the courage to motivate and guide others facing similar challenges.

We are destined to be leaders and teachers, fulfilling God's appointed purpose, much like how David's victories led him to kingship, opening doors that no other path could. Trusting in God's plan, recognizing the good He is doing, and seizing the opportunities He presents are essential, as Proverbs 3 advises:

"Trust in the LORD with all your heart and lean not on your understanding; in all your ways acknowledge him, and he will make your paths straight." - Proverbs 3:5-6

Even when others question our presence and purpose, it's crucial to keep moving forward. God will guide us if we stray, so heeding His counsel and following His lead is vital. We are in this moment for a divine purpose, and in due time, the significance of each step we take will become clear. Choosing to align ourselves with God's guidance is crucial because He has plans to accelerate our progress in the months ahead.

The Lord's teachings emphasise that trials are not arbitrary; they offer opportunities for growth, maturity, and spiritual development. Romans 5 reinforces this idea:

"And not only so, but we glory in tribulations also: knowing that tribulation worketh patience, and patience experience and experience, hope." - Romans 5:3-4

Regardless of the origin of the challenges, whether self-inflicted, imposed by external factors, or a natural part of life, our response ultimately defines their impact on our lives. When faced with trials, remember that God's grace is always available. By placing our trust in Him and accepting His grace, we can navigate challenges with resilience:

"My grace is always more than enough for you, and my power finds its full expression through your weakness." - 2 Corinthians 12:9

The Apostle Paul viewed trials as opportunities to rely on God's strength, allowing Christ's character to develop within us, leading to patience, experience, and hope.

Take comfort in the knowledge that God does not permit anything too difficult to handle without His permission and that He can ultimately bring good out of any situation:

"And we know that all things work together for good to those who love God, to those who are called according to His purpose." - Romans 8:28

Though we may not always comprehend the purpose behind our trials, we can have faith that God orchestrates everything for our ultimate benefit. Therefore, it is crucial to maintain faith and stand steadfast during difficult circumstances, recognizing that God's wisdom surpasses our own.

In summary, trials and challenges are not setbacks but opportunities for personal growth and spiritual development. God desires for us to trust Him and rely on His guidance as we navigate these trials. By embracing the journey, following God's lead, and understanding the purpose behind our experiences, we can overcome obstacles and fulfil the plans God has for us. It's through these trials that we discover our true potential, inspire others, and expedite our progress in fulfilling our divine purpose. Do not waver and play into the hands of the enemy's agenda. In Ephesians 6:10–12, it says,

"Finally, my brethren, be strong in the Lord and in the power of His might. Put on the whole armor of God, so that you may be able to stand against the wiles of the devil. For we do not wrestle against flesh and blood, but against principalities, against powers, against the rulers of the darkness of this age, against spiritual hosts of wickedness in the heavenly places."

19

Posture of Encounter : Humility

Dear brothers and sisters, in this chapter, let the message of encounter - embodying the posture of humility and draw inspiration from the Scriptures in Luke 7:36-39. Let us remember that as we gather, our major concern should be that of God and what He thinks of us, rather than what others think of us.

In 2 Samuel 6:20-23, King David served as an example, humbling himself before the Lord even when others were there. He danced with all of his strength, letting up his need for comprehension and command and embracing the thrill of God's praise. Similarly, we must be willing to surrender our own desires and agendas, acknowledging that God's ways are higher than our ways, as mentioned in Isaiah 55:9.

"For as the heavens are higher than the earth, so are My ways higher than your ways, and My thoughts than your thoughts."

As we continue on with this journey of encounter, let us also reflect on the words of David. He prayed,

"Create in me a pure heart, O God, and renew a steadfast spirit within me. Do not cast me from your presence or take your Holy Spirit from me. Restore to me the joy of your salvation and grant me a willing spirit to sustain me." - Psalm 51:10-12

May we too approach God with a repentant heart, seeking His transformation and the renewal of our spirits.

Brothers and sisters, drawing near to God requires effort and intentionality. It necessitates a conscious decision to prioritise our relationship with Him above all else. We must be willing to invest our time, energy, and resources to seek His face and experience the depth of His love and presence. Why? Because He is worth it! In Him, we find true fulfilment, peace, and purpose.

The importance of positioning ourselves for divine encounters is that just as Jacob wrestled with God and refused to let go until he received a blessing, as mentioned in Genesis 32:24-28, let us approach God with a desperate desire for His presence and intervention in our lives.

Moreover, we must be sensitive to God's timing, recognising the significance of each season and embracing His divine appointments. In Acts 2, the disciples positioned themselves in the upper room, waiting for the promised Holy Spirit. Their obedience and expectancy led to a powerful encounter with the presence of God.

Therefore, I encourage you to cultivate an unbroken focus on God, setting aside distractions and earthly concerns. Let us focus. Focus is the key to fire and impact. Let us be known as a people who are wholeheartedly devoted to the Lord, passionately pursuing His purposes and Kingdom.

Furthermore, our encounters with God should be marked by definite expectations. We must boldly approach the throne of grace, describing our needs and desires, knowing that God hears and answers our prayers. Let us not hesitate to present our requests before Him, for He is a loving and attentive Father.

Finally, let us engage in heartfelt prayers, pouring out our hearts and souls to our Lord. Let our prayers be marked by sincerity and confidence, just as Hannah ardently sought God's intervention and won favour, as read in 1 Samuel 1:10-13. May our prayers climb as delicious incense before God's throne in our search for encounter.

Beloved reader, I encourage you to embrace this posture of encounter with humility. Let us care more about what God thinks of us than the opinions of others. As we lay down our need to understand and control, draw near to Him with a willing spirit, and make the effort to seek His face, we will find ourselves transformed and renewed.

In conclusion, the lesson we learn from this chapter is that, as believers, our primary focus should be on what God thinks of us rather than seeking the approval of others. We should approach God with humility, surrendering our desires and agendas, and positioning ourselves for divine encounters. By prioritising our relationship with Him, being sensitive to His timing, and engaging in passionate prayer, we can experience His transformation and renewal in our lives. May we be known as a people who are whole-heartedly devoted to the Lord, passionately pursuing His purposes and Kingdom.

20

Encountering God's Call to Mission and Service

The sacred verses of Matthew 28:16-20 unveil an extraordinary moment between Jesus and His disciples post-resurrection. This encounter holds immense significance as it introduces God's call to mission and service, known as the Great Commission. Let's delve into this encounter and explore its transformative power.

As the resurrected Jesus stood before His disciples on a Galilean mount, awe and doubt mingled within them. Yet Jesus as Son of God, declares with unchanging authority,

"All authority in heaven and on earth has been given to me" - Matthew 28:18

With His divine authority, Jesus commissioned His followers to reach all nations with discipleship. This summons extended to all who would follow Him, an active involvement in God's redemption plan. The mission was clear: spread the gospel's transformative message, baptise believers, and teach His commands.

The following passage echoes Paul's experience on the road to Damascus, as mentioned in Acts 9:1-19. Once Saul, a fervent persecutor of early Christians, encountered the risen Christ in a blinding light, struck down and humbled, Paul heard Jesus' voice asking, "Saul, Saul, why do you persecute me?" - Acts 9:4. This encounter turned his life around, transforming him from persecutor to passionate Christ-follower.

Paul was commissioned as an apostle to share the gospel among Gentiles, kings, and Israel. His path shifted dramatically; he became a tireless missionary, enduring hardships and imprisonment for Christ's kingdom.

The encounter between Jesus and His disciples and Paul's transformation on the Damascus Road resound as timeless calls to mission and service. It transcends cultures and generations, urging us toward purpose and surrender to God's plan.

Answering God's call thrusts us beyond comfort zones into a journey demanding faith, sacrifice, and perseverance. Like the disciples and Paul, we must relinquish our ambitions for the Gospel's sake.

Consider these words: "The Spirit of the living God is guaranteed to ask you to go somewhere or do something you wouldn't normally want or choose to do. The Spirit will lead you to the way of the cross, as He led Jesus to the cross, and that is definitely not a safe, pretty, or comfortable place to be."

Remember, responding to this call isn't solitary. The Holy Spirit empowers, guides, and equips us. Through the Spirit's aid, we overcome weaknesses, enter unknown territories, and impact lives.

Let's heed the call to make disciples of all nations. Embrace the transformative encounter with God's call to mission and service, akin to the disciples on the Galilean Mount and Paul on the Damascus Road. Live with open hearts for the Spirit's guidance, surrendering to divine direction and being willing vessels.

In closing, the encounter between Jesus and His disciples and Paul's transformation serve as profound illustrations of God's call to mission and service. Reflecting on these encounters, let's courageously embrace the call, committed to advancing God's kingdom. Be emboldened by Jesus' promise to be with us always, even to the age's end, in Matthew 28:20

"teaching them to observe all things that I have commanded you; and lo, I am with you always, *even* to the end of the age."

21

Embracing the Concept of Living Sacrifice for Divine Encounter

In this chapter, let us delve into the profound notion of "living sacrifice," extending a divine invitation to a period marked by enhanced grace, humility, servanthood, and the unfolding magnificence of God's glory in our lives.

Apostle Paul, in his letter to Romans 12, advises us to offer our bodies as living sacrifices—a concept that might seem unfamiliar in our modern society but is integral to expressing our beliefs in a meaningful manner. Living sacrifice entails dedicating ourselves entirely to God, akin to the ancient temple traditions. It signifies an act of surrender, devotion, and worship where we relinquish our desires, ambitions, and will, allowing God's purpose to flow through us. It represents an ongoing commitment to seeking His will above all else, bringing honour and glory to Him through our lives.

During this period of living sacrifice, we embrace symbols of profound spiritual significance. Like butterflies undergoing transformation, God moulds us in His image, granting us freedom and a renewed identity. Our lives become a testament to His grace, spreading love and effecting positive change.

Oil, representing God's anointing and favour, symbolises our openness to the Holy Spirit's transformative work. By cleansing and purifying us and infusing us with passion and love, the Spirit works through us, becoming vessels through which His anointing flows, bringing healing, restoration, and favour.

The rainbow stands as a significant symbol of God's promises. As people dedicated to living sacrificial lives, we aim to comprehend His intentions and the path He has set for us, relying on His guidance and understanding. We gain a profound understanding of His intentions, aligning our lives seamlessly with His divine plan.

Lastly, a heart surrendered to God overflows with joy and love. This joy surpasses circumstances and this love transforms lives and communities. As living sacrifices, these qualities become our essence, radiating God's glory and drawing others to His presence.

I urge you, dear friends, to embrace this call to living sacrifice and enter a season of enhanced grace. It's a period of growth, transformation, and profound intimacy with our Heavenly Father. As you surrender, you'll experience His presence unprecedentedly, and His glory will manifest through you. Your faithfulness will result in an increase in your gifts and anointing—a season of promotion where your unity with Him becomes even more evident.

In 2 Corinthians 3:17–18, we are reminded,

"Now the Lord is the Spirit, and where the Spirit of the Lord is, there is liberty. But we all, with an unveiled face, beholding as in a mirror the glory of the Lord, are being transformed into the same image from glory to glory, just as by the Spirit of the Lord."

May this message kindle a fire within you to embrace the call to living sacrifice. Step into this promised season of enhanced grace with humility and a willingness to be used by God for His purposes. May the transformative power of living sacrifice lead you to a deeper revelation of God's love, joy, and favour.

In conclusion, living sacrifice invites us to surrender to God, becoming vessels of His glory fully. We experience transformation, freedom, and an outpouring of His grace through this surrender. By embracing the symbols and qualities of living sacrifice, we align ourselves with God's will and become agents of positive change in the world. Let us continually strive to be humble and useful servants, allowing the Holy Spirit to work through us and be a source of hope, understanding, perseverance, wisdom, revelation, joy, and love to those around us.

22

Position for Encounter

In Luke 8:40-56, we encounter two powerful stories – the healing of a woman with a blood issue and the resurrection of Jairus' daughter. These stories provide insight into how we can position ourselves for life-changing encounters with Jesus.

Desperate: Both Jairus and the woman were desperate for an encounter with Jesus. They recognized their need for miracles and humbly approached Jesus, acknowledging that only He could meet their deepest needs. Desperation is a key ingredient for positioning ourselves for an encounter with Jesus. When we realise our own limitations and turn to Him in desperation, we open ourselves up to receiving the miracles, healing, and breakthroughs that only He can provide.

Intentional: It's not enough to simply be desperate for an encounter; we must also be intentional in seeking Jesus. The woman with the blood issue demonstrated this by taking a risk and pushing her way through the crowd to touch Jesus' robe. She believed that if she could just have physical contact with Him, she would be healed. Similarly, positioning ourselves for an encounter with Jesus requires intentionality. We need to actively seek Him through prayer, reading His Word, attending worship services, and surrounding ourselves with a community of believers. By intentionally positioning ourselves in His presence, we create an atmosphere conducive to encountering Him.

Persistent: Both Jairus and the woman faced discouragement and prolonged disappointment. Jairus experienced the death of his daughter while waiting for Jesus, and the woman had been suffering for years without finding a cure. Despite these challenges, they remained persistent in their faith and pursuit of encountering Jesus. Positioning ourselves for an encounter with Jesus requires perseverance in the face of obstacles. We must learn to unclog our hearts from doubt, fear, and disappointment. God desires to heal and unclog our hearts, but it requires us to persistently hold onto faith and trust in His goodness.

Faith-filled: Faith is the fuel that propels us towards an encounter with Jesus. Both Jairus and the woman demonstrated unwavering faith in Jesus' power and ability to bring about the healing and breakthrough they desperately needed. To position ourselves for an encounter, we must fill our hearts with faith. This means choosing to silence the well-meaning voices of doubt and distraction around us and fixing our eyes on Jesus alone. We need to yield to Him, putting everything else aside and focusing on His promises and character. In doing so, we shift our perspective from fear to faith, creating an environment where encounters with Jesus become a reality.

In summary, to position ourselves for impactful encounters with Jesus, we must first recognise our desperation for His miracles and humbly approach

Him. We then need to be intentional, actively seeking Him through prayer, reading His Word, and engaging with a community of believers. Despite any challenges or disappointments we may face, we must persistently hold onto faith, unclogging our hearts and trusting in God's timing and goodness. Finally, we need to fill our hearts with unwavering faith, silence the voices of doubt and distractions, and yield ourselves entirely to Jesus. As we adopt these positions of desperation, intentionality, persistence, and faith, we open ourselves to transformative encounters with the Saviour, who can change our lives forever.

23

Navigating Life's Journey with Jesus: Insights from the Gospels

Drawing wisdom from the Gospel accounts of Matthew, Mark, Luke, and John, we unveil a multitude of insights regarding maintaining focus and unwavering commitment to Jesus. The advantages of remaining steadfast in our faith journey with Jesus, regardless of life's challenges, are both abundant and profound.

Abundance of Life: In the Gospel of John, Jesus heralds Himself as the wellspring of an abundant life. Remaining intertwined with Him, nurturing His love, and adhering to His guidance enables us to encounter a life brimming with purpose, joy, serenity, and contentment.

Divine Guidance and Clarity: Just as Jesus likens Himself to the Good Shepherd, the Gospels underscore the notion that abiding with Jesus leads to divine guidance and clarity in our journey. His teachings supply us with wisdom, insights, and discernment, steering us through challenging decisions and ensuring we remain on the righteous path.

Forgiveness and Reconciliation: Evident in the Gospel narratives is Jesus' boundless love and His willingness to extend forgiveness. By standing steadfastly by His side, we can experience the transformative power of His pardoning grace, receiving redemption for our transgressions. This bestows upon us healing, rejuvenation, and a fresh start in our relationship with God.

Fortified Faith: By closely engaging with Jesus' life, witnessing His miracles, absorbing His teachings, and ultimately acknowledging His resurrection, His disciples acquired a profound understanding of the significance of unwavering faith. Sustaining a deep connection with Jesus and embracing His teachings fosters an enduring faith that bolsters us through the trials and tribulations of life.

Everlasting Salvation: Staying resolute in our commitment to Jesus results in the ultimate reward of eternal salvation. Within the Gospels, Jesus promises eternal life to those who place their trust in Him, believe in His sacrificial act on the cross, and follow His path faithfully. This pledge of everlasting communion with God offers hope and forms a solid foundation for confronting life's challenges and uncertainties.

The collective teachings found in the Gospels of Matthew, Mark, Luke, and John emphatically underscore the significance of maintaining focus on Jesus and upholding our commitment to Him. By doing so, we fortify our faith, experience life's abundance, receive divine guidance, find redemption and forgiveness, and ultimately secure eternal salvation. These blessings empower us to navigate life's peaks and valleys with unwavering hope, inner peace, and a profound sense of purpose.

24

Deepening Trust in Jesus: Unveiling Endless Reasons to Believe

There are still numerous vital aspects and compelling reasons why we should place our complete trust in Jesus and stay unwavering on our path with Him:

Unconditional Love: Jesus epitomises unconditional love through His teachings and deeds. His love for us remains unwavering, regardless of our imperfections and faults. Trusting Him enables us not only to receive His boundless love but also to extend it to others.

Perfect Role Model: Jesus offers us the perfect example of living a righteous and purpose-driven life. His teachings on love, forgiveness, humility, and compassion serve as a guiding light for our interactions with others, inspiring us to grow more like Him.

Divine Wisdom: Jesus possesses divine wisdom and profound understanding. Placing our trust in Him and remaining connected grants us access to His insights and guidance for our life journey. His wisdom surpasses human comprehension, equipping us to make wise choices.

Comfort and Peace: Through our unwavering trust in Jesus, we discover comfort and inner peace, especially in the midst of life's challenges. He provides solace for our sorrows, healing for our wounds, and the assurance of His constant presence.

Source of Strength: Jesus is our unshakeable source of strength. When we encounter difficulties, temptations, or trials, relying on Him empowers us to overcome them. Trusting in His strength enables us to endure and mature in character.

Transformative Power: Trusting Jesus and remaining committed to His path opens us up to His transformative power. He possesses the remarkable capacity to reshape our hearts, minds, and lives for the better. Through Him, we experience personal growth, healing, and restoration.

Eternal Hope: Jesus extends to us the gift of eternal hope. By placing our trust in Him, we find confidence in the promise of everlasting life and a future in the presence of God. This hope sustains us during moments of uncertainty, reminding us that our ultimate destination extends beyond our earthly existence.

My dear friends, there is still so much more to discover about Jesus and compelling reasons to continue placing our wholehearted trust in Him. His unconditional love, role as the perfect exemplar, divine wisdom, ability to bring comfort and peace, role as our enduring source of strength, transformative power, and the eternal hope He bestows are all powerful incentives. Wholeheartedly trusting in Him allows us to experience His full presence, guidance, and blessings in our lives.

25

Trusting God in Challenging Seasons: Lessons from Psalms 23:4 and 37:3

In life's journey, we all face valleys and challenging seasons that test our faith and resilience. As we navigate these difficult times, the wisdom of David in Psalms 23:4 and 37:3 provides profound guidance.

"Yea, though I walk through the valley of the shadow of death, I will fear no evil; for You are with me; Your rod and Your staff comfort me." - Psalms 23:4

"Trust in the LORD, and do good; Dwell in the land, and feed on His faithfulness." - Psalms 37:3

Owning the Season

David, a man after God's heart, teaches us that challenging times are not our destined end. We must not let these seasons define us; instead, we should embrace them, acknowledging the pain while trusting God's purpose. The key lies in owning the season without letting it own us. Despite the challenges, we are not failures or disqualified; rather, these trials are opportunities for God to shape and train us.

Trusting Amidst Challenges

During trials, we often question God's intentions and are tempted to walk away, especially when worldly success eludes us. However, David's insight in Psalm 37:3 reminds us to trust God and continue doing good. In challenging times, our natural tendency might be to withdraw, seeking comfort in temporary pleasures or self-pity. Yet David encourages us to dwell in the land and feed on God's faithfulness.

Feeding on His Faithfulness

Feeding on God's faithfulness means keeping company with His unwavering love and promises. Instead of turning to worldly distractions or negative thoughts, we should settle down and keep company with His faithfulness. Just as we seek comfort in familiar foods or habits during difficult times, we must find solace in God's unchanging character.

Reflection and Transformation

Reflecting on past challenging seasons allows us to see how God shaped us during those times. Understanding that every season offers an opportunity for God to work in our lives changes our perspective. We no longer view challenges as hindrances but as stepping stones for growth and transformation.

Reframing Difficult Seasons

If you've felt defined by a challenging period, it's time to view it differently. Recognize that God desires to shape you through those moments. Instead of seeing yourself as a victim of circumstances, see yourself as a warrior, emerging stronger and wiser after each battle.

Every season, no matter how challenging, is an opportunity for God to mold us into His image. Let us trust in Him, acknowledge the purpose of our pain, and keep company with His faithfulness. As we do, we can emerge from the valleys of life not broken but refined, resilient, and deeply rooted in faith. The miracle of every season is our ability to continue to trust God in that season.

26

Nurturing Faith : A Guiding Light for you and me, Seekers of Jesus

Maintaining faith in Jesus Christ is not just a personal endeavour but also a beacon for those seeking spiritual enlightenment. Scripture offers invaluable verses, guiding our faith and fortifying our trust in God's presence.

In 1 Chronicles 10:13, we learn the consequence of unfaithfulness: "Saul died for his unfaithfulness; he was unfaithful to the Lord by not keeping His command and seeking guidance from a medium."

This underscores the importance of unwavering faithfulness to God.

In 2 Corinthians 1:24, the collaborative nature of faith community shines: "We don't dominate your faith but work together for your joy because you stand firm in your faith."

This verse emphasises the strength found in a supportive faith community.

James 2:17 offers a profound truth: "Faith without works is dead."

This challenges us to translate our faith into meaningful actions, highlighting the vitality of active faith.

Revelation 14:12 encourages steadfastness: "the endurance of the saints, those who keep God's commandments and hold fast to Jesus' faith."

Perseverance in faith is emphasised, urging us to adhere to the teachings of Jesus.

Psalm 121:7 assures us of divine protection: "The Lord will guard you from all evil; He will preserve your soul."

This verse serves as a comforting reminder of God's watchful presence, especially during trials.

In 1 Peter 1:8-9, the profound joy of faith is illuminated: "Though you have not seen Him, you love Him; and even though you do not see Him now, you believe in Him and rejoice with an inexpressible and glorious joy, receiving the outcome of your faith, the salvation of your souls."

This emphasises the deep joy and assurance found in faith.

Romans 8:28 provides solace in challenging times: "All things work together for good for those who love God, who are called according to His purpose."

This verse offers comfort, affirming God's providence even amidst adversity.

As you continue your spiritual journey, these verses stand as wellsprings of encouragement and strength. Remember, faith is not solitary; it thrives within a supportive community of believers, a fundamental aspect of your spiritual quest.

27

Conclusion: Embracing Jesus' Transformative Message

In this odyssey through the life and teachings of Jesus Christ, we delved into the heart of His transformative message. Navigating ancient texts and timeless wisdom, our goal was not just comprehension but internalization of these profound teachings.

Jesus, a figure of immense historical and spiritual importance, transcends mere theological doctrine. He becomes a guiding light in our complex lives, offering a universal roadmap. His message, boundless in its love and compassion, extends beyond cultural confines, uniting humanity in its entirety.

Love and Compassion: The Core of Transformation

At the heart of Jesus' transformative message resides love - an unconditional love that knows no bounds. It calls upon us to extend compassion to our fellow beings, to be the menders of broken souls, the listeners in times of need, and the understanding hearts that bridge divisions. Through His teachings, we unearth the transformative potency of love, a dynamic force that repairs fractured relationships, nurtures wounded spirits, and unifies fractured communities.

"And now these three remain: faith, hope, and love. But the greatest of these is love." - 1 Corinthians 13:13

Forgiveness and Redemption: The Path to Healing

Jesus imparts the profound art of forgiveness, a balm in a world often plagued by grudges and retribution. His message paves a liberating path through the act of forgiveness, enabling us to shed the shackles that tether us to our past. In forgiveness, we find redemption and freedom, kindling inner peace while laying the foundation for collective healing and renewal.

"Bear with each other and forgive one another if any of you have a grievance against someone. Forgive as the Lord forgave you." - Colossians 3:13

Faith and Trust: Anchoring Through Life's Storms

Throughout His teachings, Jesus underscores the significance of faith and trust in a higher purpose. In moments of desolation and doubt, faith serves as our unwavering anchor, a constant reminder that even amid life's tempests, a guiding light shines. Trusting in the divine plan empowers us to navigate life's tribulations with tenacity and optimism, recognising that each experience, be it joyful or sorrowful, contributes to our spiritual growth.

"Trust in the Lord with all your heart and lean not on your own understanding; in all your ways submit to him, and he will make your paths straight." - Proverbs 3:5-6

Living a Life of Purpose: Embodying Transformation

Ultimately, Jesus beckons us to live a life infused with purpose. It's a life where our actions harmonise with our convictions, where kindness becomes our lingua franca, and where empathy moulds our interactions. Embracing the transformative message of Jesus is not merely an intellectual endeavor; it's a resounding call to manifest these teachings in our everyday existence.

"He has shown you, O mortal, what is good. And what does the Lord require of you? To act justly, to love mercy and to walk humbly with your God." - Micah 6:8

As we conclude this profound exploration, let us carry the essence of Jesus' transformative message forward. May His teachings inspire our thoughts, resonate in our words, and imbue our deeds. In our unique ways, let us contribute to a world that mirrors the love, compassion, and empathy that Jesus exemplified. In embracing His message, we unearth not merely a guide for today but an eternal wisdom that lights our path toward a more compassionate, forgiving, and purposeful tomorrow.

28

Jesus' Transformative Touch : Personal Testimonies

In a world where scepticism often shrouds ancient texts, the Bible emerges not merely as a collection of historical accounts but as a living, transformative force. It's easy to dismiss these narratives as antiquated, yet within their pages lies a profound power capable of reshaping lives that even penetrates deep into our souls, revealing truths we might not have even been aware of.

A Call to Witness

These personal testimonials stand as living proof that the Bible's power transcends time. They invite us to witness the incredible, to embrace the living, breathing essence of its words. Let these stories serve as a reminder: the Bible isn't just ancient history. It's a source of transformative power, waiting to touch our lives in ways we might not have imagined. So, let's open our hearts, read these accounts, and allow Jesus' transformative touch to resonate within us.

Hebrews 4:12 states, *"For the word of God is alive and powerful. It is sharper than the sharpest two-edged sword, cutting between soul and spirit, between joint and marrow. It exposes our innermost thoughts and desires."*

In the words of Psalm 107:2

"Let the redeemed of the Lord tell their story."

Our voice matters, and our stories have the potential to bring hope to those seeking God.

PERSONAL TESTIMONIES UNFOLD:

Guided by Faith: A Journey of Divine Providence and Community Transformation #1

In 2011, my husband and I faced a significant relocation from Bunbury to Perth after six years of settling down in a regional area. Thankfully, our company provided temporary accommodation in the bustling CBD for a month, allowing us time to adjust to this new city.

With hope and anticipation, we diligently explored the metropolitan area, seeking a strategically located residence near the city or airport, considering my husband's FIFO work schedule. However, after attending a fellowship gathering in the Southern suburbs, like Canning Vale, and experiencing the lengthy drive back, we decided these areas were too far from the city centre. So, we focused on the Northern, Eastern, and Western suburbs, which seemed more promising. But as the weeks passed, the rental market became intensely competitive, with countless applicants vying for each property we viewed. Rejections piled up, and we faced the disheartening possibility of being left homeless.

As the term for our temporary accommodation came to an end, a sense of urgency and desperation consumed us. We had believed that God guided us to relocate to Perth, but now the idea of seeking divine intervention to find a home seemed unexpected. Nonetheless, in our profound desperation, we fell to our knees and cried out to our Heavenly Father, seeking His help.

In that moment of need, we recalled a recommendation from a pastor and her daughter from FCC the previous week. They had suggested a new suburban area called Piara Waters, which was even further south than Canning Vale. Although enchanted by a beautiful house there, we dismissed it due to its rental fees exceeding our budget. However, after pouring out our hearts to God, we decided to trust in His guidance completely. Miraculously, the very next day, the rental price for that house had significantly dropped, aligning perfectly with our financial limitations. We wasted no time and applied immediately, securing the house without any other competing tenants.

Yet the story's tapestry extends beyond our personal aspirations. As we settled into our new home, we discovered that our neighbours hailed from my husband's cherished hometown, Kota Kinabalu. It became evident that this encounter was far from a coincidence; it was God's divine purpose at work. Over two years, we built a genuine and amicable relationship with our neighbours, especially Emilia and her family. Though they were Catholic, they attended church sporadically. Driven by God's love, I prayed for them and offered continuous support.

Through unwavering invitations, fervent prayers, and God's grace, Emilia's family responded and began attending church services regularly. Eventually, we purchased a home in Canning Vale, right next to theirs, two years after they committed to regular worship. Witnessing their remarkable spiritual growth, Emilia and Leonard are now esteemed leaders in our Connect group, embodying the transformative power of God in their lives.

Reflecting on this incredible journey, I'm humbled by the profound truth that God's ways are higher than ours. In our most desperate moment, God orchestrated a series of events, leading us unerringly to the perfect dwelling and using it as a catalyst to impact the lives of our neighbours. This powerful testimony serves as a poignant reminder that God's faithfulness and provision go beyond our immediate needs, reaching the hearts and souls of those around us. I am eternally grateful for His unwavering guidance and bear witness to His goodness and indescribable plans for each of us.

Throughout this remarkable journey of finding a home and transforming lives, we learned the invaluable lesson of trusting God wholeheartedly. In moments of desperation and uncertainty, when our own efforts seemed futile, we surrendered our burdens to God and relied on His divine guidance. It was through this complete trust and surrender that God revealed His sovereignty, orchestrating events in a way we could never have imagined.

Proverbs 3:5-6 sums it up : "Trust in the Lord with all your heart, and do not lean on your own understanding. In all your ways, acknowledge Him, and He will make straight your paths."

Additionally, Psalm 37:5 reassures us: "Commit your way to the Lord; trust in Him, and He will act."   This sentiment assures us that entrusting our desires to God results in His intervention, working things out for our ultimate good.

Ultimately, this journey has taught us that trusting God to the end not only brings us closer to His will but also allows us to play a part in the fulfilment of His purposes. By faithfully following His lead, we become instruments of transformation and blessings in the lives of others, just as we witnessed with Emilia and her family.

This journey taught us that trusting God unconditionally not only aligns us with His will but also allows us to impact the lives of others. By following His lead, we become instruments of transformation and blessings, as witnessed with Emilia and her family. As we navigate life's uncertainties, let us remember the powerful lesson of unwavering faith. Surrendering to God's guidance and plan leads us to places we could never reach alone, profoundly impacting both our lives and the lives of those around us.

God of Grace: My Protector and Provider #2

I grew up in an average and fragmented family. Despite being the favoured firstborn, my family was broken, with my mother working tirelessly to support us. My father was minimally involved, leaving me to navigate life on my own. However, amidst the chaos, attending church every Sunday was a constant in my life.

During my teenage years, I found myself drawn back to my mother's church, where I served as a pianist in the English congregation. Without formal training, I trusted and obeyed, firmly believing that God equips those He calls. My simple faith allowed me to grow and explore music beyond what I had learned through training.

While serving in the music ministry, I experienced the infilling of the Holy Spirit. His presence became my mentor, guiding me to improve my skills and understand music on a deeper level. With the help of inspiring speakers and a supportive community, I flourished in my spiritual journey.

Like any teenager, I faced temptations and challenges. I engaged in secret relationships, finding solace in the freedom of my unhealthy family dynamics. However, God intervened when my tire punctured as I drove home, reminding me of His perfect love. It was a wakeup call that made me realize the importance of transparency and true love, which brought me closer to God.

Although I resolved to serve the Lord faithfully, I still struggled with materialism and pride. These struggles impacted my academic performance, but through God's grace, my mother was able to fund my education in a twinning program near our home. This opportunity taught me the value of independence and reliance on God's provision.

Living independently in Adelaide presented a chance for genuine intimacy with God. With the distractions of my previous city removed, I could lose myself in His presence. Through playing the keyboard gifted by my sister, I discovered contentment in Him alone. It was during this time that I composed several songs, realising that God had put a new song in my heart.

As I immersed myself in seeking God's guidance, my materialistic tendencies began to fade. Every decision, including finding a life partner, was submitted to His will. Contrary to my initial desires, God brought someone from a humble background into my life. This experience humbled me and taught me to rely solely on God's provision and obediently follow His guidance.

My journey has shown me that focusing on and trusting God until the end, paves the way for His intended path in our lives. God's grace has protected me and provided for me, even in the midst of a fragmented family and personal struggles. Through faith, obedience, and seeking Him above all else, I have learned that true contentment and fulfilment can only be found in God alone.

https://youtu.be/S2oGHaKpq-Q?si=ERpkS1ke6ScvamPG

Faith Tested, Faith Restored: A Journey Through Trials and Divine Intervention #3

2022 has been a roller coaster and challenge filled year for many, including our family, to say the least. In the early months of the year, I was fully recharged. Launching what God has placed in my heart to start a prayer meeting group with deep worship as the central goal, it started very well. During that time, God has used the relationship that I had with my core prayer partner to bring deliverance to a parent of my student from her depression and to help her stabilise emotionally. Things were happening on a high note and my heart was filled with great anticipation of what God was doing. However, it all came to a sudden halt with the coronavirus incident catching up on me in May.

It was a usual music rehearsal on Saturday and I didn't realise I had caught the virus from one of the members until I couldn't get out of bed three days later. The day before my symptoms worsened, I had inadvertently organised a facial for my aunty and her daughter, so that was it. My worst nightmare had happened! Not because Covid- I was not afraid of it. But it was the fact that I have infected someone else that made that thought unbearable to me. I was guilt stricken to the point of blaming God for what had happened. I told my husband that I did not want to live anymore because of the guilt. The thought subsided a little after being chastised by him for making such a horrendous comment.

But wave after wave came, while I was still reeling from grogginess the next day and giving online lessons, a text came, which laden me with much more guilt as there has been some sort of misunderstanding from a prayer partner that I have breached some confidentiality. I felt choked and overwhelmed the whole night right after receiving the text, as I was feeling so bad for myself once again.

That night in bed at the lower deck bed, as my heart was hurting and my head was aching severely, tears couldn't stop rolling down and I was trying to hold back my groan as my son was laying down on the upper deck, ready to sleep. I was lamenting in my heart to God, 'Oh God, why is this happening to me? Where are you? When have I been faithful to you all these years, serving you tirelessly since my youth, giving my all to you? Please God, I cannot take it anymore. I am going to quit! I'm giving up all my ministries. Music, kids, prayer, witnessing, etc.!'

And suddenly, my ten year old son broke out, 'Do you love me'? I didn't think much but replied almost immediately, 'Yes,' why? He then replied, 'Feed my lambs'." I didn't pay much attention; I thought he was just joking, as he always does. Then he asked again, 'Do you love me?' And I replied unhesitantly, 'Yes, of course I love you!' Why are you asking me this?! My son replied, 'Tend my sheep." There was silence. And he wanted to ask again for the third time. This time, I got it! Yes, yes, I get what you're telling me, Lord!! (John 21 : 15-19) Tears continued to roll down as my loving Saviour would speak to me through my son and respond to my cry at that instant! My aching heart and head were relieved and I fell asleep peacefully that night. It was so comforting to hear this from God through my son.

The next few days or weeks were when I felt God directing me back to Bible Study Fellowship again as I realised my own fragility without the support of a community. I knew I needed a community of believers to be able to continue to stand strong. Just before I could settle back in, not surprisingly, I was asked to take up the role of Children's Leader. Without hesitation, I took it on despite my already busy working schedule and church ministries on weekends. Because my answer to Him was 'Yes, I love you.'

As if this wasn't enough, more intense trials and afflictions like a mighty flood came upon my parents toward the end of the year, where they were threatened by loan sharks because of my prodigal brother, wiping out almost everything and every ounce of their being. But again, His faithfulness never fails and the storm soon became still. And being grounded in the community of BSF'ers and studying God's word , His word has always been so timely and accurately aligned to the circumstance I was in. That is another story to tell.

I know this is not the end of the destination and that there will be many more challenges to face ahead, but I will continue to trust in the name of the Lord, who will deliver me out of all troubles, and my soul shall wait and hope in Him. Like the psalmist song

"If it had not been the Lord who was on our side, when men rose up against us:

Then they had swallowed us up quickly, when their wrath was kindled against us: Then the waters had overwhelmed us, the stream had gone over our soul: Then the proud waters had gone over our soul. Blessed be the Lord, who has not given us as prey to their teeth. Our soul is escaped as a bird out of the snare of the fowlers: the snare is broken, and we are escaped. Our help is in the name of the Lord, who made heaven and earth." —Psalms 124

"He also brought me up out of a horrible pit, out of the miry clay, and set my feet upon a rock, and established my steps." - Psalm 40:2

https://youtu.be/Rv9dZ0O0NCw?si=eLEb5XCuN506RGEK

By Grace Loh of FCC; Perth, Western Australia

Overcoming Challenges and Experiencing Miracles: Personal Testimonies from the Pandemic Time #1

The emergence of the COVID-19 pandemic ushered in unparalleled challenges, compelling individuals worldwide to confront various hardships. In the midst of these trying times, I encountered two profound testimonies that not only tested my resilience but also deepened my faith in the transformative power of prayer and the unexpected miracles that grace our lives.

In September 2019, tragedy struck my family in Kedah, Malaysia, with the passing of my eldest brother. Complicating matters, his son had left behind an incomplete will, creating a complex legal situation. My wife and I assumed the role of administrators, entrusted with the task of ensuring a fair distribution of the estate, particularly for my niece. The journey to resolve these matters proved to be daunting and intricate.

Determined to find resolution, we sought legal assistance and ventured into a rigorous legal battle, fortified by our unwavering faith and ceaseless prayers. With each hurdle, our persistence and belief in the power of divine intervention grew stronger. The journey was marked by numerous follow-ups, late-night discussions, and an unwavering commitment to seeing it through.

Following countless follow-ups and a prolonged legal battle, our perseverance bore fruit. In August 2022, we received the news we had been desperately waiting for—the estate was finally settled. The long and arduous process had reached its end, marking a significant triumph over adversity.

This journey taught us the importance of unwavering faith, perseverance, and unity in the face of adversity. In the wake of tragedy, we stood strong, facing legal challenges with determination and hope. The victory achieved in August 2022 stands as a testament to our resilience and the power of unity in the pursuit of justice and closure.

A Testament to God's Comfort: Triumph Over Grief & Healing #2

In the depths of my sorrow, I found peace in the unwavering presence of God. In this testimony, I will share an experience of navigating the loss of my beloved wife Seok Lian, who passed away on November 22nd, 2022, due to acute pancreatitis during our vacation in Rome, Italy, finding strength in God's grace amidst the grief.

During Seok Lian's three-week hospitalisation in Rome, I faced numerous challenges, particularly language barriers. Yet, God's grace manifested in unexpected ways. I am deeply grateful to the Italian government for their compassionate care, provided without charge, even to foreigners like us. The prayers of my fellow believers and the assistance of the Embassy of Malaysia were instrumental during this difficult time. Their support helped me overcome communication hurdles and translate essential documents, ensuring understanding with insurance companies, banks, and local authorities.

Amidst these trials, I received a pre-diabetic diagnosis in June 2022, influenced by my family's history of diabetes. Despite the genetic predisposition, I chose to believe in Jesus' healing power. Through extensive research, I adopted various strategies to manage my blood glucose levels. Each morning, I faithfully consumed a teaspoon of organic Ceylon cinnamon powder in warm water, maintained regular exercise, controlled my sugar and carbohydrate intake, and fervently prayed for Jesus' healing touch. My dedication bore fruit; my HbA1C tests in June 2022 and December 2022 showed significant improvement, with a reading of 5.3% in June 2023. The doctor confirmed I was no longer pre-diabetic, a testament to Jesus' healing grace and power.

In these moments of trial and healing, I am reminded of Isaiah 53:5, "By His stripes, we are healed," and 2 Corinthians 12:9, "My grace is sufficient for you, for My strength is made perfect in weakness." To God, I offer all the glories, honours, praises, and thanks, acknowledging His unwavering support and grace in my life.

By Jeremy Tay of Calvary Community Church in Gelang Patah; Johor, Malaysia

A Journey of Faith and Healing:My God, Who Never Forsakes Me

It was the morning of March 30, 2023, when I found myself battling severe diarrhoea, fever, and stomach cramps. My initial thought was, "Oh no, not another flare-up of my Eosinophils (EOS), a type of white cell!" I underwent a blood test, which revealed that it wasn't my EOS acting up but rather an infection. I visited a GP clinic and was prescribed medication, assuming it was probably food poisoning and that I would recover soon. Unfortunately, my condition worsened, and I had to be admitted to the A&E department of a local hospital in Johor Bahru.

After five days, I was discharged, but my body remained weak. The fever and diarrhoea returned, and I noticed I was struggling to breathe. Consequently, I was readmitted to the same hospital. With the administration of antibiotics and various tests, my condition improved, and I was discharged after eight days. However, the doctors couldn't determine the exact infections I had contracted. A week later, I was still weak, unable to walk even short distances. Another blood test revealed that the infections were still present. Frustrated and desperate, I questioned God, wondering why He hadn't healed me. I had been suffering for almost a month, seeking guidance on what to do next.

For the past five years, I have been consulting with a haematologist doctor at Singapore General Hospital (SGH) regarding my rare blood disorder. Upon receiving the distressing blood results, I consulted her again and was presented with the option to undergo treatment in Singapore. Despite being aware that I would be subjected to higher medical fees as a foreigner, I hesitated. However, I felt a prompting to proceed, knowing that I could stay at my sister's house while in Singapore. The plan was to receive outpatient treatment from a recommended Infectious Disease Consultant (ID) for my infections. So, on April 27, I crossed the border.

On May 1, my doctor insisted that I admit myself to the A&E department of SGH when my blood pressure suddenly dropped to 80/50. My condition appeared to have worsened, as I still had a fever, diarrhoea, and swollen feet. While in the ward, I had my first consultation with the ID doctor. Due to my weakened state, I required a blood transfusion, and numerous blood tests were conducted. Once my blood pressure stabilised, I was discharged.

Unfortunately, bad news arrived swiftly after my discharge. On the same day, the ID doctor called and informed me that I had contracted a fungal infection. I had to undergo an MRI, a brain scan and lumbar puncture procedures. The following day, I learned that I also had a viral infection, which necessitated my readmission to the hospital ward for treatment. By then, I was already experiencing bloody diarrhoea. The doctor explained that my immunosuppressed state had made me susceptible to these infections, which, if left untreated, could be life-threatening. I received treatment through medicated drips and oral tablets. Four days later, on May 12, I was discharged from my fourth hospital admission. Today, God has healed me!

Where was God during those weeks of suffering? Why was He silent? Before I travelled to Singapore, I was constantly drowsy and unable to pray much due to a fever. However, when I began feeling better in Singapore, I knew that God had not forsaken me or left me in my situation as said in

"The Lord Himself goes before you and will be with you; He will never leave you nor forsake you. Do not be afraid; do not be discouraged." - Deuteronomy 31:8

During my first stay in the SGH ward, I found it difficult to sleep at night. From another ward, I could hear a man screaming for two hours, along with delirious shouts from a fellow ward member. Unable to tolerate the distractions any longer after one night, on the second night, the Holy Spirit spoke to me: "Bind the spirit behind the shouts!" I obeyed, and soon I was binding the spirit of KuanYin, aka, goddess of mercy, and the spirit of death. The shouting subsided, and I managed to get some sleep.

On the night before I was discharged during my second SGH admission, the Holy Spirit once again prompted me to share Jesus with two other wardmates. Both ladies were battling cancer—Madam K had lymphoma, and Madam L had blood cancer. Although my command of Mandarin was limited, I couldn't find peace until I decided to obey. I shared about Jesus and prayed for both of them. I urged Madam K to call upon Jesus, as she was enduring intense pain from chemotherapy. Madam K expressed interest in knowing Jesus, but Madam L hesitated due to family traditions. I continue to pray that they will both accept Jesus one day. The seed of salvation has been sown!

I was deeply concerned about my medical expenses at SGH. With numerous tests, procedures, and other admission costs, I questioned whether I could afford the higher fees as a foreigner. One night, while lying in my hospital bed, the Spirit of God spoke to me, urging me to let go of anxiety and worries. He assured me that He was my Provider, and indeed, He had already provided even before my SGH treatments. When I was hospitalised in Johor Bahru, one of my brothers, whom I shall call WS, visited me from Singapore. Before he left, he informed me that he had deposited a sum of money into my Singapore bank account. As I was too ill to check the amount, I didn't know how much he had deposited. When the SGH bills arrived, I discovered that the total amount was exactly the same as the deposit made by WS. Isn't God wonderful and marvellous? He already knew, and He provided it in advance.

During my consultations at SGH with the haematologist and ID doctors, I only had to pay one consultation fee. Both doctors agreed to charge only one fee. I recognized that this was made possible by God's favour

"For You bless the righteous, O Lord; You cover him with favour as with a shield." - Psalm 5:12

God is good all the time! All the time, God is good!

Throughout my illness, my church and friends prayed for me. God brought many people into my life who cooked for me, bought food, kept me company, and even a Christian sister who purchased prescribed medication in Johor at a much lower cost. I praise the Lord for the service of His body, the Church. Their acts of kindness deeply touched me. I remember a sister who sent me an encouraging message, urging me to focus on God's word rather than my physical symptoms. I began reading Psalms daily and allowed the Word to minister to me and bring healing.

I have never endured illness for such a prolonged period in my life. Consequently, I questioned the Lord as to why I had been suffering for almost two months. God spoke to me through

"But we also glory in our sufferings because we know that suffering produces perseverance; perseverance, character; and character, hope." - Romans 5:3-4

I learned the importance of perseverance and glorifying God even in the midst of suffering.

Lesson Learned: Throughout this difficult journey, I learned that even in times of suffering and uncertainty, God is with me. He never forsakes His children, and His presence brings comfort and strength. My faith was tested, but I discovered that God's faithfulness remains unwavering. He provided for all my needs, both physically and financially, and surrounded me with a supportive community of believers. I experienced the power of prayer and witnessed God's healing touch in my life. Moreover, I learned the value of obedience to the prompting of the Holy Spirit, even in challenging circumstances, as it can lead to opportunities to share the love of Jesus and plant seeds of salvation in the lives of others. My suffering taught me perseverance, character, and hope, and I now understand the importance of glorifying God even in the midst of trials. Through it all, I have come to rely on God more deeply, knowing that He is always with me, guiding me, and bringing beauty out of ashes.

Anonymous, Malaysia

A Testimony of God's Faithfulness and Provision #1

Our God is faithful and full of goodness. He sent the Holy Spirit to comfort and encourage me during times of overwhelming fear. Today, I want to share a testimony that exemplifies God's unwavering presence in our lives. It serves as a reminder that no matter how dire our circumstances may seem, God remains faithful and provides for His beloved children.

Last year, I surprised my mother, and her tearful reaction will forever be etched in my memory. However, at that time, I was facing financial difficulties and felt lost. Despite my financial constraints, I yearned to visit my family and decided to return home. Unfortunately, this decision led to accumulating credit card debts.

Seeking God's Guidance: Realising my mistake, I repented and asked God for forgiveness. I began to place my trust in Him, knowing that He would guide me through the challenges ahead. I reminded myself that God never promised an easy or smooth life, but He promised to be with us always. Through prayer, worship, Bible reading, and devotion, I witnessed God leading me back on track, step by step.

Debt Redemption and Abundance: God's boundless love granted me an opportunity to pay off all my debts in April 2023. To my surprise, not only did I manage to clear my debts, but I also had more than enough resources to embark on exciting travels to Malaysia, Bangkok, New Zealand, and even back to Malaysia for a second time in June. God's provision was abundant and undeniable.

Trusting God's Promises: During the months of March and April, God reassured me not to fear about my son's school fees and encouraged me to continue doing His work in Malaysia in June. Although confusion and struggles crept in, I held onto my faith, knowing that God would make a way. He is the way, the truth, and the mighty One. As Hebrews 11:6 reminds us, without faith, it is impossible to please God.

The Miracle Unveiled: Upon returning from my recent trip to Melbourne, I eagerly asked my husband about our expenditures during our Malaysia trip. Astonishingly, he informed me that we spent nearly 6,000 AUD dollars, yet we had no debts on our credit cards. It left me bewildered, contemplating how this could be. It was nothing short of a miracle.

Lesson Learned: This testimony serves as a powerful reminder that regardless of the circumstances we face, God is always there to fulfil His promises. When we obediently follow His instructions, He demonstrates Himself as a God of provision. We need only to have unwavering faith and trust in His divine plan. Let this testimony inspire us to put our faith into action and to remember that God never fails His beloved children.

Another testimony I would love to share with you : Miraculous Healing that exceeded all expectations #2

In March 2022, I experienced a terrible incident that caused me severe mental and physical pain. On that day, I was attempting to cook one of my husband's favourite dishes, deep-fried Korean rice cakes. Unbeknownst to me, the fire was turned to the maximum, and within a short period of time, the rice cakes absorbed an enormous amount of heat. As I approached the pan to flip the rice cakes, some of them suddenly exploded, and boiling oil splashed onto my neck and left forearm, causing major burns. Immediately after the incident, I rushed to a nearby medical centre to seek medical attention.

During the initial assessment, the doctor informed me that the burn was quite severe and prescribed a strong painkiller to help me endure the pain. He also warned me that, despite the painkiller, I would likely experience a great deal of pain during the night. When I returned home, I bowed down to the ground and started to pray and praise. Although the pain in my neck prevented me from singing "Hallelujah," I decided to hum the rhythm of a song of praise instead. At that moment, a scripture came to my mind: Luke 9:1, "Jesus called all his disciples to give them power and authority over all evils and cure all diseases."

As I declared and proclaimed this scripture, I realised that I could start singing with significantly less pain. I continued singing, and my voice grew louder and louder. The song I was singing was "Peace Like a River." Miraculously, I was completely healed just two days after the incident.

The lesson I learned from this experience is the importance of trusting in God until the end. Despite the intense pain and uncertainty, I chose to turn to God in prayer and praise. I found peace in His Word and declared it with conviction. By putting my trust in God, I witnessed a miraculous healing that exceeded all expectations.

In conclusion, this testimony serves as a reminder that even in the face of adversity, trusting God and seeking His comfort can bring about unexpected blessings.

By Deborah Tan of Hillsong Church, Victoria, Australia

The Lord is my shepherd; I shall not want

In 2015, merely a year into my marriage, the weight of life's pressures began to bear down on me.

As a newlywed couple, my husband and I encountered a multitude of challenges. Our differences led to countless disputes, escalating into a growing sense of resentment and animosity between us. As my marriage teetered on the edge, my career also left me adrift. Having left my full-time job, I embarked on a freelance journey as a wedding stylist, only to find my business struggling and myself steeped in uncertainty.

During this tumultuous period, I began to experience anxiety attacks for the first time. Sleepless nights and the fear of solitude enveloped me in a suffocating grip. I became hypersensitive to sounds, easily distracted by noise, and found myself trapped in an unfamiliar emotional space. Each day seemed to plunge me deeper into an inescapable sadness.

A diagnosis of anxiety disorder followed, compounded by hormonal imbalances that brought additional health challenges. It felt as if my world was crumbling around me. My road to recovery included a six-month course of medication, during which I had to step back from work and concentrate on healing. The side effects of the medication regimen were notable. Upon taking the medicine, a sense of relaxation would wash over my mind, providing the much-needed calmness I sought. However, it came at the cost of hindering my ability to recall specific details from many past events. Additionally, remembering the intricacies of daily conversations posed a challenge, thereby affecting my capacity to perform more complex tasks effectively.

Amidst the chaos, a glimmer of hope emerged. Clinging to God's promises for myself and my family, I recited a verse from Psalms 23 that had resonated with me since childhood:

"The Lord is my shepherd; I shall not want.
He makes me to lie down in green pastures;
He leads me beside the still waters.
He restores my soul;
He leads me in the paths of righteousness
For His name's sake."

In moments of anxiety, tears in my eyes, I would whisper, "Lord, lead me to those green pastures and still waters..." and a wave of peace would wash over me. I sensed His presence, knowing that I stood in the company of my King and Shepherd.

During my recovery, I sought solace in sermon podcasts that focused on Jesus's finished work on the cross for me. I meditated on how the Lord bore my burdens and sorrows on the cross, and through His wounds, we find healing (Isaiah 53:4-5). Anchoring myself in His words, I boldly proclaimed that my healing was secured and embraced this gift of restoration.

Meanwhile, I embraced a new path, working part-time as a children's art teacher and a florist. These uncomplicated roles brought me comfort, and small victories bolstered my spirits. Although my journey had taken an unexpected turn, I trusted that the Lord would eventually lead me to those green pastures. Three months into my role as a part-time florist, a breakthrough occurred. My employer extended a full-time offer, promoting me to a creative consultant role in a new department. It was a remarkable shift, one I had never foreseen, and I recognised that only divine intervention and grace could have brought it about.

On a different note, a profound transformation was also underway in my relationship with my husband. By regularly immersing ourselves in the gospel, we discovered the strength to embrace each other, imperfections and all, under the protective canopy of the Lord's grace.

My mental well-being gradually improved as I immersed myself more and more in God's word and the promises He had tenderly bestowed upon me. Six months into my medication journey, I made a resolute choice to entrust my complete healing to God, thereby relinquishing my reliance on medication. With a systematic approach, I began reducing my dosage while unwaveringly affirming the efficacy of the completed work on the cross. Astonishingly, I discovered an increasing ability to grapple with intricate tasks and effectively manage my responsibilities. In turn, this newfound proficiency led to a well-deserved pay raise while also fostering strong connections with both my employers and the creative team.

By this juncture, six months into my medication journey, I had moved beyond its reliance. Though occasional bouts of sadness still surfaced when challenges emerged, I had a potent recourse. I would turn to the Lord, immersing myself in worship and rejuvenating my spirit by listening to gospel sermons that focused on the all-encompassing significance of the Lord's finished work. This profound truth, resonating within me, served as a catalyst to uplift me from my bout of depression. I am acutely aware that there exists immense power within His words.

Eight years have swiftly passed; I no longer depend on any medication. My mental well-being has been fully restored. My marriage journey is far from a continuous bed of roses, but with the Lord's promises, such as "Surely goodness and mercy shall follow me all the days of my life…" (Psalm 23), I no longer rely solely on my limited wisdom to communicate with my spouse. In moments of adversity and need, I turn to my Lord and Saviour, seeking refuge under His wings and within His shelter (Psalms 91). In the presence of my Shepherd, I always find rest, followed by spirit-led action.

Over the years, my husband and I have discovered better ways to communicate, drawing us closer to each other. Having weathered numerous challenges together, we've forged a more resilient bond than we ever thought possible. We express profound gratitude to the Lord Jesus Christ for His divine intervention in our lives and His boundless love for us. I would not be where I am today without the Lord's unwavering guidance and His comforting presence.

By Emma Chong of New Creation Church, Singapore

By divine appointment

It was the year 1988 when I first accepted Jesus as my Lord and Saviour. I remembered the warm and wonderful feeling in my heart as I stood in front with a few others and prayed the sinner's prayer. That started my thirty plus years journey of walking with the Lord. The Lord guided me and led me to grow from a young babe in Christ to a follower of Jesus, continuing to change me from the inside out. The growing process was full of challenges and difficulties, but the Lord was always faithful to pick me up and sometimes carry me through those times when I felt so helpless and defeated.

The miracles He performed in my life were so real and mind boggling! Looking back, God is always in control. He arranged for me to meet my Christian friend in my new school. I saw how she spoke enthusiastically about Jesus. I never knew such a personal god from my Roman Catholic background. I went to her church activities one day where a pastor gave an altar call for people to accept Jesus. It was where I gave my life to Jesus.

Later, when I received the JPA scholarship to further my studies, I moved to Kuala Lumpur from Kuantan. There I met with more Christian friends and was able to attend church. After much prayer and deliberation for a month since I became a Christian, I called my mother about my change in faith. I received an earful from my mother who threatened to disown me. After that I didn't call back for two weeks. Little did I know God had miraculously worked His way through my staunch Roman Catholic mother and my laidback father in Kuantan which led them to receive the Lord Jesus Christ as their Lord and Saviour! Later on my brothers also accepted the Lord Jesus Christ as their Lord and Saviour.

Other miracles that God had done in my life were how He arranged for my meeting with my husband through my pastor. The astonishing part was that my husband saw me a few weeks earlier in a healing rally arranged by the church where I was one of the helpers on stage. After that he couldn't find me until my pastor gave him my phone number to meet up. Apparently, my pastor had been praying for us before our introduction. My husband and I got married in November 1998 after a year of courtship.

Next, the long persevering wait (six years) for our first child. I actually took the step of faith to quit my job before I got pregnant, much to the dismay of my supervisor at MFRD SEAFDEC, Singapore. During the waiting period, I had my prayer warrior mother and sisters in Christ who prayed together with me to be pregnant. I did my quiet time every morning and went for healing rallies, visited traditional chinese medicine clinics and gynaecologists during those six years.

There was no sign or word from God until one morning in February, 2004, I was reading Psalm 113 until verse 9 - which states He will settle the barren woman as a happy mother of children. The whole words just shone so brightly that my tears poured down my eyes. I knew that God has promised me I will have a child and not one, but children. Immediately, I called my husband to tell him that God will bless us with a child. Through what means, I don't know, but He will do it. I wrote it down in my diary as a step of faith in God. Lo behold, I was pregnant a month later.

Now I am a mother of three children, ages 19, 17 and 13. My journey of being a stay at home mother all this time is filled with many prayers and trust in God's leading and guidance. Proverbs 22:6 - Train up a child in the way he should go; even when he is old he will not depart from it. This verse is so true when I see how my 3 kids grow in their relationship with God. I try to play my part in exposing them to things regarding God through prayers, bible reading, memorising verses, and using my life as an example of growing in the Lord.

Finally, I end with these verses in Ephesians 3:20-21

"Now all glory to God, who is able, through His mighty power at work within us, to accomplish infinitely more than we might ask or think. Glory to Him in the church and in Christ Jesus through all generations, forever and ever! Amen."

By Esther Cheong of Church of Praise; Johor Bahru, Malaysia

A Divine Turn : From Desperation to Faith

I vividly recall my baptism, which was on Easter Day in 2014, an occasion witnessed by joyous friends with whom I celebrated. As a new believer then, my devotion to God remained passive. Despite my consistent Sunday attendance at Church, my heart and mind remained fixated on worldly desires rather than the Kingdom of God. My energies were consumed by pursuing my ambitions and ascending the corporate hierarchy. This self-absorbed pursuit eventually led me to a new city and an appealing career opportunity, brimming with excitement and grand aspirations. Along this path, I entered a relationship that brought me happiness, making life appear perfectly orchestrated.

However, life took an unexpected turn, leading me down a harrowing spiral. Abandoning my career, I found myself a single mother, overwhelmed by feelings of loss, shame, helplessness, and heartbreak. In the darkest moments, I was even tempted to end my life, peering out my apartment window with the intent to leap. Yet, a providential intervention stayed in my hand—an adjacent church building that caught my eye. It was as if God's touch reached my heart, igniting a torrent of tears. In that vulnerable instant, I cried out to God for help, a plea born from the depths of my soul.

As I approached the final stages of pregnancy, my water broke while I slumbered alone. In the grip of fear, realising my impending labour, I turned to God in prayer, invoking the comforting words of Psalms 23:4

"Though I walk through the valley of the shadow of death, I will fear no evil; for you are with me; Your rod and Your staff, they comfort me."

Remarkably, an encompassing peace enveloped me, and serenity prevailed throughout my labour.

A turning point emerged when a compassionate woman extended an invitation to attend church. Astonishingly, this invitation was extended by none other than the very church situated right across from my apartment—a convergence too uncanny to be mere happenstance. In that moment, clarity dawned upon me; God was orchestrating this encounter to draw me closer to Him.

Through days of adversity, it was God who bore me through. My unwavering anchor lay in the words of 2 Corinthians 12:9 :

"My grace is sufficient for you, for My strength is made perfect in weakness."

Amidst the global pandemic, an unforeseen opportunity emerged in my career—a directorship position presented itself unexpectedly. Surrendering control of my life to God had not only opened my eyes to His omnipresence but had also extricated me from the clutches of brokenness, fear, and anxiety.

Each morning now dawns with a heart overflowing with gratitude and joy, an embodiment of the transformation God has wrought. No longer do I rely on my own striving; rather, I have entrusted my life into the capable hands of God. It is this unyielding trust that compels me to share my journey with others, so that they too may come to know the boundless joy that God offers. Living life to its fulness, the aboundance grace from God. In the wisdom of Proverbs 3:5-6, we are reminded:

"Trust in the Lord with all your heart, and lean not on your own understanding; in all your ways acknowledge Him, and He shall direct your paths."

Anonymous, Malaysia

Healing thru Prayers A Testament of Faith

I wanted to take a moment to share a testimony that has deeply impacted me. In late June, 2016 my husband's job required us to relocate to Johor. Shortly after the move, around mid-August, I started experiencing troubling episodes of vertigo.

Concerned, I visited a clinic and began taking medication. Unfortunately, my condition did not improve and, in fact, worsened over time. Seeking further medical attention, I consulted with an ENT specialist who admitted me to the hospital. The neurologist/physician also evaluated my condition, conducting various tests such as blood tests, MRIs, ECG, X-rays, and an echo.

Surprisingly, all the results came back normal, without any signs of abnormalities. The neurologist discharged me with a slightly improved condition, attributing my symptoms to some form of vertigo, although unable to provide a definitive diagnosis. In search of a second opinion, I consulted another doctor recommended by my general practitioner, which led to additional medications as we explored every possible avenue for my recovery.

A week later, while my friend that i knew for many years, was visiting; a frightening incident occurred. Within a span of just two hours, I experienced six episodes of fainting. Alarmed, she instructed my daughter to call my husband for immediate medical assistance. Once again, I found myself back in the hospital, hoping for answers.

However, despite thorough examinations, the medical professionals remained unable to identify the root cause of my symptoms. Even the ENT specialist ruled out inner ear imbalance as a potential cause. Instead, he suggested a sleep study (which yielded clear results) and advised me to see a medical doctor who specialized in surgical interventions. This led to a cycle of more medications, further complicating my situation.

Throughout this challenging time, a few friends suggested that my condition could have a spiritual component. At first, I lightly brushed aside their suggestions, but their persistence led me to consider the possibility. This prompted me to seek treatment at Mount Elizabeth Hospital in Singapore, based on my friends' recommendation to consult with doctors there. Similar to my previous experiences, I underwent assessments from heart, ENT, and neurology specialists. Due to the severity of my symptoms, I was placed in the High Dependency Unit (HDU) as a precautionary measure. More tests followed, including EEG (which scanned brain waves) and a CT scan. To my surprise, one of the neurologists even suspected the possibility of seizures or epilepsy.

Despite the extensive medical examinations, the scientific explanations fell short in providing a definitive answer for my condition, leaving many gray areas. I visited three different hospitals, consulted with three different teams of doctors, and underwent numerous tests such as MRIs, X-rays, ECG, CT scans, EEGs, and blood tests. Yet all the results showed no signs of underlying issues. Each time, I was discharged with a slight improvement in my condition but with additional medications. However, even at home, I continued to experience dizziness, fainting spells, and falls when seated, sometimes multiple times a day. With that, I also thank God that every time that happened, I was not on the staircase, walking up and down the house, or even in the shower. At times, I ask, "Hello God, are you there?"

"Are you watching over me?" And so I would not be disheartened as He showed me a guardian angel. I feel a big angel protecting me all the time.

As there was nothing I could do about the condition, we attributed these symptoms to the stress of our recent relocation and the transitional period we were going through. Or even a medical condition that science couldn't explain.

In the midst of uncertainty, I found peace in my faith. It reminded me of the words from Psalm 3:5-6, which say, "I lie down and sleep; I wake again because the LORD sustains me. I will not fear though tens of thousands assail me on every side." Throughout this entire journey, God has been my sustainer and protector. To Him be all the glory, for no man can claim credit for this miraculous healing.

Then, on a Sunday morning, my husband and I attended the service at Paya Lebar Methodist Church in Singapore on October 9th. At the request of our friend from the UK, Pastor Irene prayed for my healing. Coincidentally, our friends from the UK, Maggie, John, Suzie, and Quek, were also present that day.

In the moment Pastor Irene prayed, I experienced an immediate clarity in my head. The heaviness and headache vanished, and since that prayer, I have not experienced any dizziness or fainting spells whatsoever. In fact, I even resumed driving on October 13th, despite being advised to wait until my review on October 24th. I have also contacted my doctor to discuss reducing the medications before the review. All praise be to God for His remarkable work in my life!

This entire experience has taught me a valuable lesson – that God's power transcends the limitations of medical science. When faced with unexplained circumstances, it is crucial to seek divine intervention and place our trust in His plan. My journey serves as a reminder that through prayer and faith, remarkable healing and restoration can occur. May we all find encouragement in turning to God in times of need and witnessing His miraculous work in our lives.

Thank you for your patience in reading this lengthy sharing. May God bless each one of you abundantly.

"I lie down and sleep; I wake again because the LORD sustains me. I will not fear though tens of thousands assail me on every side." - Psalm 3:5-6

"Trust in the LORD with all your heart and lean not on your own understanding; in all your ways submit to him, and he will make your paths straight." - Proverbs 3:5-6

By Karyn Chua of Kingdomcity; Western Australia

Chosen by God to the journey of the unknown #1

"You did not choose me, but I chose you and appointed you so that you might go and bear fruit—fruit that will last—and so that whatever you ask in my name, the Father will give you." - John 15:16

I am a Chinese Malaysian, growing up in a broken family that worshipped idols. My father had an affair, which caused my mother's marriage to suffer, leading to her developing a mental illness. Despite these challenges, my mother's love raised me and my siblings. Due to our impoverished condition, I couldn't afford to buy meat during high school. I learned to use a slingshot to hunt birds or catch squirrels for food. We didn't have gas at home, so we would collect dry branches from the forest to use as firewood.

Regarding worship, I worshipped all kinds of gods, but I had never worshipped Jesus. Since I was young, my mother took me to temples to offer prayers to bodhisattvas. She named me "Guan Xiang." Even though I have become a pastor today, people from the countryside still call me by that name. Among friends, I also learned the practice of inviting spirits into my body, but I was unsuccessful. The incense burned my skin, leaving some scars.

At the age of 21, I followed a friend to Singapore to work in construction. I earned money during the day and attended an electronics technology course at night. The construction industry was tough, especially when climbing up and down tall buildings in Singapore was extremely dangerous.

I rented a house in Bukit Panjang, and sometimes when I opened the window, I would see a lovely girl from the opposite house. Unbeknownst to me at the time, she was a Christian. One day, her younger brother handed me a form inviting me to join the youth camp of their church. I thought this was my chance to pursue her, so I took a few days off work to attend their church camp.

To be honest, my motivation was not to find Jesus but to find a girlfriend, specifically the beautiful girl I often admired through the window. During my first participation in the church camp, I found the people there to be very friendly. Being a young Malaysian, my skin was darkened by the intense sun, and at that time (1977), flared pants and long hair were in fashion. I even had a love charm in my wallet! But no one looked down on me or made me feel embarrassed; those few days gave me a sense of acceptance and love.

Not only that, the church's songs attracted me, the testimonies of Christians moved me, and most importantly, Pastor Hu Minqi's preaching illuminated me, a typical sinner. When the pastor called for the young people who hadn't accepted Christ to raise their hands and make a decision, I struggled for one or two days. On the third day, the last day, I finally raised my hand to express my faith in Christ. I knew my motivation for joining the camp was not pure, but God's love is greater than my flaws. He chose me to be His child (John 1:12)

Allow me to share some changes in my life after accepting Christ:

I quit smoking, drinking, and gambling. I no longer went to nightclubs or danced with bar girls.

I stopped using foul language.

I received the Holy Spirit within me, replacing the evil spirits that used to dwell in me. I experienced true peace and joy.

I enjoyed participating in various gatherings and worshipping the holy, supreme, and omnipotent God.

God's love touched me and inspired me to share the Gospel with others.

Previously, I lost money gambling, but after accepting Christ, I used my limited resources wisely.

The senior pastor mentored us and gave us the opportunity to serve in church activities such as children's Sunday school.

Previously, I neglected my mother, but after accepting Christ, I fulfilled filial piety by caring for and loving her.

In terms of relationships, the pastor advised me to work hard and save money. The sister in question was still in high school, so it was not appropriate to influence her studies.

The inner calling from the Lord became clearer and clearer, making me feel that He was calling me to full-time ministry.

A Journey of Faith and Dedication: Serving God and the Community #2

1977-1981: The Calling and Confirmation After being born again in the Holy Spirit, there was a noticeable change in my life. Under the guidance and nurturing of the head pastor, I began to practise a life of spiritual devotion, children's Sunday school, fellowship, worship, financial offerings, training, distributing pamphlets, and bearing witness to the Lord by spreading the gospel. The Lord prepared me for four years of full-time ministry in Singapore, and within me, a strong desire to follow the Lord wholeheartedly began to emerge. At the time, I was working as an air conditioning technician in Jurong, and I became deeply concerned about the souls of my colleagues, leading them to the church to meet the Lord's warmth. One evening in 1981, I experienced the Lord's calling. Unable to sleep, I turned to Isaiah 53:1-12 in my devotional time, and the Lord's Spirit spoke to me through this passage. For several hours that night, I was deeply moved, continuously shedding tears and praying, dedicating myself to the Lord's use. After the Sunday service, I told the pastor about this, and he responded by saying that he had also wanted to ask me about my desire for full-time ministry. Being a Malaysian, the pastor arranged for me to be equipped for full-time ministry at the Malaysia Bible Seminary in Kuala Lumpur.

1982-1987: Theological Training and Lifelong Partner Due to impoverished circumstances, I didn't graduate from Form 5, which was a basic requirement for theological college. Dr. Tan Soon Theng, the college principal, admitted me as a probationary student. Studying theology was extremely challenging for me because of my limited prior education and the long gap since I had last been in school. The reading assignments, essays, and other requirements were daunting, and I contemplated giving up. However, the Lord comforted me with 2 Corinthians 12:9-10, assuring me that His grace was sufficient for me and that His power would help me in my weakness. Thanks to the Lord, I graduated from theological college after four years of hard work and practical training in the church. I entered seminary at the age of 24 and graduated with a theology certificate at 28. In my third year, at 27, I met my current spouse, Pastor Huang Meigui. She enrolled in 1984, and despite her darker skin resembling that of indigenous people from mountainous regions, she was a beautiful young lady. I thank the Lord for giving her to me as my lifelong partner in ministry and as a virtuous helper.

1987-2023: Missionary Work, Marriage, Church Purchase, Ordination, Further Education, Community Outreach, and Northern Malaysia Mission

After graduating from seminary in 1987, I returned to the mother church in Singapore to serve as a pastor while expressing gratitude to my mother church, C.G.M. (Christian Gospel Mission).

In July 1987, the Lord led me to return to Johor, Malaysia, specifically Kulai, in the southern part of West Malaysia, where I planted a church, now known as K.V.C (Kulai Vision Church). I was sent as a missionary by J.V.C (Johor Bahru Vision Church).

On January 9, 1988, I married Pastor Meigui, and God was with us. The number of believers in Kulai Vision Church increased, and the church purchased a building. I was ordained as a pastor, and God blessed us with three children, one daughter and two sons. Every six years, we had a sabbatical year with a salary, so the Lord Jesus provided opportunities for further education, from theology certificates and diplomas to a bachelor's degree and a master's degree in pastoral ministry. Some people advised me not to go to Kulai, south of West Malaysia, for mission work, saying that the people there were stubborn and hard to convert to Christianity.

However, before going, the Lord had given me a verse from 2 Corinthians 5:

"For we walk by faith, not by sight." - 2 Corinthians 5:7

I thank the Lord that over the years, not only have more people come to faith, but at least ten young people have entered full-time ministry. All glory belongs to God, as we are merely His workers, and without His grace, we would accomplish nothing.

From 2005 to 2023, the Lord gave us a vision to start the Kulai Children's Home, where we have been able to care for orphaned and underprivileged children from broken families. Starting with one orphan, we now have approximately 30 children in the home, along with a dedicated team of co-workers.

"A father of the fatherless, a defender of widows, Is God in His holy habitation." - Psalm 68:5

Our heavenly Father is the God of orphans and widows, and He loves them. Three of the children have had the opportunity to attend university. We thank Sister Belle and her husband for their support, as well as Sister Karyn Chua and her husband for helping us acquire an apartment building for the children's home and provide accommodation for our co-workers and the orphans. We pray that the Lord will reward them for the wonderful work they have done for the Lord's sake, and all glory belongs to God.

From providing food to Gerik, Perak, to mission work, the Lord is faithful and abundant, just as Matthew 6:33 promises: "But seek first the kingdom of God and his righteousness, and all these things will be added to you." We heard the cry for food from a distant place, and my wife and I drove from Kulai to Gerik, Perak, a journey that takes 8-10 hours, to share surplus food from the Children's Home with the indigenous people in the northern mountainous areas of Malaysia.

Later, God led us to begin sharing the gospel with the few Chinese residents there. From 2019 to 2023, we have arranged bi-monthly short-term mission trips to Gerik. Thanks to the Lord, even before and during the pandemic, this poverty-alleviation and mission work has never stopped. The Lord promised that when He opens a door, no one can shut it.

Hence, My journey is a testament to my unwavering faith and dedication to full-time ministry. I experienced a profound calling in 1981, leading me to serve the Lord wholeheartedly. Despite facing educational challenges, I pursued theological training and met my lifelong partner, Pastor Huang Meigui. Together, we embarked on a mission to Kulai, Malaysia, where we planted a church, cared for orphaned children, and conducted community outreach.

All glory through His grace, Luke 17:10 reminds us:

"So you also, when you have done all that you were commanded, say, 'We are unworthy servants; we have only done what was our duty.'"

By Senior Pastor Chong of Kulai Vision Church; Kulai, Malaysia

A Tale of Faith and Redemption : Journey from Despair to Divine Intervention

My name is Huang Yanping, from Yongping, Johor. I am the eldest daughter in my family, and I have two younger brothers who are 6-7 years younger than me. My father is a local, while my mother is an Indonesian Chinese. Before I came to faith, I experienced three valleys in my life. From the age I can remember, around 5 years old, my parents often argued. My father was heavily involved in alcohol and gambling, often taking out his anger on me when he was drunk, using a cane to beat me. I lived a life of being constantly beaten and scolded, knowing that whenever he drank, I was bound to be beaten that day. He was also addicted to gambling, especially when I was 8 years old.

Around that time, my mother couldn't bear my father's temper and left, her whereabouts unknown. My father was emotionally devastated, drank even more heavily, and squandered the family's once comfortable assets. When my mother left me, I felt deeply hurt and saddened. Seeing my father's decline, I felt lost and uncertain about my future. That was the first valley in my life.

At the age of 9, our family went bankrupt, and our house was taken away. To escape, my father entrusted me and my two brothers to two different caregivers. My caregiver's family ran a small food stall business. Every day after school, I would return home at 2 PM, take a shower, do household chores, and then head to the stall to help at 3:30 PM. My tasks there included making and serving tea, packing food, sweeping the floor, washing cups, and selecting vegetables. Sometimes, I wouldn't get back home until 1 AM due to closing the stall. My grades suffered greatly during that time since it was impossible to juggle both work and studies.

On weekends, I had to help hang clothes to dry; with six people in their family plus me, I had to finish drying seven sets of clothes all by myself. I often got scolded for being slow, especially with the heavier adult clothes. I carried the burden of being dependent on others until I reached 6th grade. I was nearly at the point of giving up on myself. My father didn't want me, and my mother didn't want me either. I envied my classmates, who had happy families and didn't need to work like I did. I felt inferior and isolated, thinking I didn't belong in their world. This was the second valley in my life.

In 6th grade, my father developed kidney disease and depression, requiring medication for sleep. Ironically, this situation brought my brothers and me back together. Life was tough at that time. The four of us lived in a small room above a shophouse, sometimes eating just rice with soy sauce and eggs. With government assistance, our living conditions improved a bit. When I was 13, my brothers and I started attending church and got to know the Lord Jesus Christ. However, my faith foundation was not yet stable. Just when I thought the difficult days were behind me, my father started gambling again and accumulated a significant debt he couldn't repay due to his illness. I ended up working at a friend's restaurant to help pay off the debt, enduring gossip and rumours along the way. I despised both my father and mother at that time. There was no warmth between us, and I felt like I was born to repay debts, resenting them for not giving me a complete family and burdening me with so much pain. I felt stripped of my freedom and dignity in front of others. My life hit its lowest point at the age of 15.

One day, my father picked me up from work and told me he wasn't feeling well. He had trouble breathing, a situation that had happened before and led him to the hospital. I urged him to go to the hospital, but he insisted he was fine and told me to rest. Exhausted, I went to bed. At around 3 AM, he woke me up, saying he couldn't breathe. I called a ride-sharing service as it would take time for an ambulance to arrive.

By the time we were on the way to the hospital, his breathing had worsened. Halfway to the hospital, he passed away on my shoulder. My mind went blank. I couldn't hold back the tears until we reached the emergency room. The driver was kind and didn't charge me. The doctor informed me that my father couldn't be saved. I felt utterly helpless. It was 4 AM, everyone was asleep, and I didn't know whom to contact.

In a daze, I searched through my father's contacts and found a volunteer named Penny. I couldn't recall who she was exactly, but I remembered she had helped us before. I believe it was God's guidance. She answered the call, learned about the situation, and rushed to the hospital without hesitation. I will never forget the first thing she did when she got out of the car – she embraced me tightly and helped me handle everything. After arranging everything, she arranged for my brothers and me to stay at a children's home, where I met the wonderful family and Pastor Rose.

Initially, I resisted and felt like I was going from one cage to another. Little did I know, the children's home would become a turning point in my life. Here, I deepened my relationship with the Lord Jesus Christ and received baptism and much biblical training.

Pastor Rose invested wholeheartedly in me. Whenever I needed extra classes, she readily arranged them for me, providing things my parents had never prepared for me. I am grateful for not letting down those who had helped me. I achieved satisfactory results in my SPM exams, and now I am attending a great university.

What I want to express is that God never left me. He was present in visible and invisible ways, sending many angels into my life. What seemed like curses in the past have turned into blessings in Christ, as

"and we know that all things work together for good to those who love God, to those who are called according to His purpose." - Romans 8:28

Our God is loving and faithful, caring for His children and never abandoning them. Although I've experienced many hardships and harboured bitterness and resentment, I now believe ....

"that if anyone is in Christ, he is a new creation; old things have passed away; behold, all things have become new." - 2 Corinthians 5:17

By Huang Yanping of Kulai Vision Church; Kulai, Malaysia

Triumph Through Trials: A Journey of Faith and Perseverance

Our life as a married couple stands as a testament to our enduring faith and unwavering determination in the face of numerous challenges.

New Beginnings and Unexpected Challenges

In the late 90s, as newlyweds, we embarked on a journey full of dreams and hopes for the future. However, life had different plans. Our joy at purchasing our first home coincided with the onset of the Asian financial crisis. Amidst the economic turmoil, in 1997, my wife faced a challenging pregnancy with our first child, confining her to bed and adding emotional and financial strain to our young family. Just as we felt things couldn't worsen, I lost my job. We found ourselves in a perfect storm: a new home, a complicated pregnancy, a growing family, and financial instability. With unyielding determination, I seized a job opportunity in Suzhou, China, where God's grace guided us through this challenging period.

Navigating Cultural Shifts and Professional Challenges

Our journey led us through diverse Chinese cities, each presenting unique cultural and professional hurdles. Concerns about our children's education guided us back to Singapore in 2002, where the company offered a relocation during the Bird Flu pandemic, a decision we attribute to divine guidance. In a demanding work environment where I needed to give my work attention almost 24/7, my commitment to family and faith were tested. Despite the hurdles, we chose to rely on God's provision, prompting me to resign from my job. Through God's provision and glory to Him, we returned to Suzhou in early 2004.

Workplace Challenges and Divine Interventions

In a new company, I faced intricate workplace dynamics, from favoritism to corruption, leading to my departure. Yet, God's faithfulness prevailed. After reconnecting with my former employer, I was given the opportunity to rebuild their engineering department in China. Despite the challenges, I persevered, navigating the professional maze with God as my guiding light.

Embracing Change and Seeking a New Path

Starting a new chapter in 2008 with another factory in Kunshan, we felt a calling to move to Australia after two years. Despite exploring various avenues, acceptance into a university in Perth became our beacon of hope. Trusting that God had a plan, I completed my studies. However, opportunities seemed elusive, and blind corners met us at every turn. A former company reached out to me and offered to return and establish their new factory in Zhuhai. Through faith, I returned to China to contribute to building this new factory in 2013.

When the ZhuHai factory was completed and my son reached his compulsory military age for Singaporeans, God provided a position, and I was reposted to Malaysia in 2016. This move brought us closer to my son and my aging mother-in-law, now in her late eighties. God's grace allowed my wife to spend more time with her before she returned to the Lord in 2017. In 2018, an industrial incident occurred at the plant, leading to my retrenchment and marking the beginning of my crisis with the company.

Finding Strength in Crisis

The loss of my job was a heavy blow, yet it marked a turning point. In the face of adversity, we turned to our faith in Christ and family from my

Connect group. God's grace became our guiding force, providing us with unwavering strength and resilience. Simultaneously, during the pandemic, God's hope emerged, leading to the successful reinstatement of my wife's permanent residency in Australia after an absence of 25 years.

As we tread this new path, we place our trust in His divine plan, understanding that every trial has shaped us into the resilient individuals we are today. In each challenge, we have felt God's unwavering presence, molding our journey and imparting invaluable lessons of faith, perseverance, and hope. Our story isn't just one of trials; it's a powerful testament to the victory of faith over adversity, reminding us that even in the darkest moments, the light of faith can guide us to triumph.

"1 James, a servant of God and of the Lord Jesus Christ, To the twelve tribes scattered among the nations: Greetings. 2 Consider it pure joy, my brothers and sisters, whenever you face trials of many kinds, 3 because you know that the testing of your faith produces perseverance. 4 Let perseverance finish its work so that you may be mature and complete, not lacking anything. 5 If any of you lack wisdom, you should ask God, who gives generously to all without finding fault, and it will be given to you." - James 1:1-5

By Edmond Chua of KingdomCity Church; Western Australia

The God of Yesterday, Today and Forever more: The Goodness of God

Even in our old age, when the hairs turn grey and life seems to slow, God reassures us through Isaiah 46:4:

"Even to your old age, I am He, and even to grey hairs, I will carry you! I have made, and I will bear; even I will carry and deliver you."

In these words, we find solace in the unwavering faithfulness of God. His presence knows no bounds. He stands close to the vulnerable among us— be they young or old, male or female, facing disadvantage or any challenge. The promise is clear: He will never abandon us, supplying all our needs according to His divine will and purpose. In times of trial, we are called to surrender and trust, for at every moment, God is there, guiding us through life's twists and turns.

I recently experienced the depth of God's sustaining power during a time of profound grief. Just six months ago, my husband of nearly 50 years departed this world to be with his Creator. In the midst of my sorrow, God reminded me of His role as my eternal partner. Isaiah 54:5 became a beacon of comfort:

"Your Maker is your husband, the Lord of hosts is His name, and your Redeemer is the Holy One of Israel; He is called the God of the whole earth."

This chapter, rich in wisdom, took on new meaning for me. It concluded with a powerful promise in verse 17:

"No weapon formed against you shall prosper, And every tongue which rises against you in judgment You shall condemn. This is the heritage of the servants of the Lord, and their righteousness is from Me," says the Lord.

God's role as a protector and provider for the vulnerable echoes throughout the Psalms:

"He is a father of the fatherless, a defender of widows. Is God in His holy habitation. God sets the solitary in families" - Psalm 68:5.

Amid my pain, I asked, "How does God wish to work through me to support others undergoing challenging times?" Surely, He had a purpose for me in this new chapter of life. But what was it?

In response to an invitation from dear friends for a month-long trip to Israel and parts of the UK, I sought divine guidance. I needed to hear from the Lord. With prayers and the support of my children, I embarked on this journey. In Israel, on what would have been our 50th wedding anniversary, God spoke through fellow believers, confirming His plan for my new season. Prophetic words rang out, aligning with what God had whispered to my spirit long before this trip.

In particular, the words of an Indonesian pastor resonated: "The Lord is taking away the spirit of grief and giving you the oil of Joy and Peace." These confirmations were not isolated; they echoed the truth of Isaiah 26:3-4:

"You will keep him in perfect Peace, whose mind is stayed on You because he trusts in You. Trust in the Lord forever, for in Yah, the Lord is everlasting strength."

God is SO Good and NEVER fails us when we earnestly inquire of Him! I got three confirmations in one month and more were yet to come. Praise the Lord.

Throughout this journey, my favorite song, "The Goodness of God," became my anthem. Its lyrics captured my heart: "I love You, Lord, for Your mercy never fails me. All my days, I've been held in Your hands... I've known You as a Father, I've known You as a Friend, and I have lived in the Goodness of God. Your Goodness is running after, it's running after me..."

In the face of loss and uncertainty, God's goodness prevails. His presence and promises sustain us, guiding us through every step. As I reflect on these profound experiences, I am reminded that God's faithfulness knows no bounds. Through grief and joy, His love remains unwavering, a beacon of hope and a source of unending strength.

By Margaret Varughese of KingdomCity Church; Western Australia

From Darkness to Redemption: Suicidal to set Free

In 2017, while in year 12, I started experiencing ill mental health. I began having panic attacks and withdrawing from my social settings. I began experiencing a low mood and struggling to find joy in anything I did. I began to sleep a lot more and rarely left the house. In March, I started taking antidepressants to help with my low mood; however, things did not improve. In June, I experienced my first crisis when I presented to my counsellor some medication I was planning on using to end my life.

She took me to the emergency department, where I was questioned, discharged, and referred to an outpatient clinic that night. The next few months looked like weekly doctors and psychiatric appointments. Until August, when I presented to the emergency department once again in crisis. Within a few hours, they admitted me to the youth mental health ward, where I went on to spend the next two weeks.

During this time, I was diagnosed with Emotional Unstable Personality Disorder, generalised anxiety, and major depressive disorder. While in the mental health ward, I attempted to end my life once again and began engaging in self destructive behaviours to manage my emotions.

During my stay, my dad thought it would be beneficial for me to move to Brisbane to live with my aunt. Me being knee deep in avoidance behaviour, I agreed, dropped out of year 12, packed my bags, and flew to Brisbane.

That didn't last long, as my aunty was unable to cope with my issues that were still present even in another state, and back to Perth I flew. As I landed, I was hurried back to the mental health ward, where I spent a further three weeks. Over the next few months, I was in and out of the psychiatric ward regularly in crisis, having done something to endanger my life.

In February of 2018, I made the bold step to ask my school if I could go back and repeat year 12. They agreed, and I began studying with the year previously below me. It was a hard year, and many days were spent at home in bed, but my goal was just to complete year 12.

In June of that year, the mental health ward I had previously been a patient at explained that they could no longer provide treatment for me. My mum and I began looking at other places. After one day in the psychiatric house, I left as I was too overwhelmed by the other patients. I found myself at a private psychiatric hospital.

Here I spent eight weeks receiving daily therapy and medication changes. I went on to graduate from Year 12 that year (massive win!)

During 2019, I spent a lot of time in the psych ward, was diagnosed with bipolar type 2, and started mood stabilising medication and lithium. I began going through electroconvulsive treatment (ECT) and TMS (transcranial magnetic stimulation); however, the more these treatments didn't work, the more sessions I had, which led to memory loss and cognitive issues.

However, at the time, I was desperate.

In 2020, things went downhill, as the psychiatrist I had been under stated that I had treatment resistant depression and would either die or be on medication for the rest of my life. My mum stated that was not her daughter's story, and we went to find a new psychiatrist. My mum called a few mental health places, but I had gotten a reputation for being a hard patient and many organisations refused to take on such a high risk client.

Finally, a psychiatrist accepted me and after my first session, he admitted me to the psychiatric facility. However, I had snuck in a sharp object and as soon as I was left alone, I attempted to end my life. This resulted in a full lockdown of the facility and the ambulance being called on me. I woke up in a hospital, not knowing which one.

I was left in a mental health observation suit with nothing on me, not even my own clothes or my phone. I was refused entry back to the mental health ward. The psychiatrist had admitting rights to another mental health ward, which I was quickly admitted to.

This ward gave me hope and I spent two weeks engaging in therapy and seeing a rise in my mental health. However, one night I hit a low and after being refused medication to calm me down, I absconded, sneaking out, asking a cleaner to let me out and ran away to end my life. A few hours later, I was found by police and my mom in an alleyway in bad condition.

I was taken to the ED and treated. Once again, I was refused entry to another psychiatric facility and the psychiatrist had to release me from his care as he no longer was able to allow me inpatient rights to any psychiatric facility. The next few weeks were a blur and I started drinking and getting involved with the wrong crowd.

One night I drove to multiple chemists and bought all the medication I could. I found myself on a jetty, attempting to end my life yet another time. It was horrible. After calling the life line to alert them that a dead human body would be on this jetty (I didn't want a morning walker to find me), they located my whereabouts (because I had a file and my history) and were able to contact my mum, who found me. She drove me to the ED, where I had a NG tube placed and antidotes pumped into my body. Once I was medically cleared, I was transferred to a state psychiatric locked ward. It was here that I attempted to leave and was put on the Mental Health Act. I cried constantly and didn't leave my bed for 24 hours.

I felt so out of control, lost, alone and hopeless. No one in Perth would help me and no one believed I could be helped. It was in this very bland room with no privacy and no door knobs that I cried out to Jesus. I wrote these words "My heart hurts so much. It breaks my heart that I was sectioned. I don't even know how to tell people I want to cry every time I think of it, because that is so low for me. My rock bottom has hit rock bottom. This is the surface on which I grow, flourish and strive for stability, health and peace in my life.

"Rock bottom was the solid foundation on which I rebuilt my life. Let's do this, Heleema, all in for recovery, all in for Jesus. You got this, I'm ready. "

And from there, I began to crawl upwards. Slowly but steadily. The Mental Health Act was released, I went back to a private ward and I began seeing hope once again. I stopped self harming, I joined a church and I started studying. Six months later, I had weaned myself off all my medication and was truly feeling free. Now, I no longer identify with any of the diagnoses I once had. I no longer suffer from thoughts of harming myself.

Here are just a few simple things that really helped me on my journey:

Genuine Community

I owe my recovery to those who stood by me, especially my mother and my church community. When I returned to church, wonderful people entered my life. They cared genuinely, reached out, and prayed tirelessly. I decided to make KingdomCity my home church, stepping far out of my comfort zone. I joined the young adult community, attended midweek services, and connected with a group. After a long search for belonging, I finally found my place and my people.

Daring to be Vulnerable

Philippians 1:14 has become a cherished verse for me:

"And because of my chains, most of the brothers and sisters have become confident in the Lord and dare all the more to proclaim the gospel without fear."

Vulnerability isn't my natural state, but the knowledge that my testimony strengthens others' faith motivates me to share the goodness of God in my life. I shared my story at KingdomCity's New Year's Eve Prayer Praise Party and was overwhelmed by the outpouring of love and gratitude.

Seeking God's Embrace

Real change began when I fully surrendered to my heavenly Father, inviting Him into every facet of my life—my spirit, my soul, and my mind. He embraced me with love, restoring my wholeness. I stopped heeding the negative voices and rejecting the peace and joy the enemy sought to steal.

Helping Others, Healing Myself

In the middle of last year, I felt a calling to mentor the next generation and became a youth leader. At first, I felt inadequate and unworthy due to my past struggles. However, during a conversation with the youth pastor, I heard a crucial message: "God will use you as He changes you." Despite still being on medication and attending regular support sessions, I began serving and spending Fridays with remarkable young people. Shifting the focus from my problems and feelings to theirs brought a greater sense of purpose.

Finding My True Identity

Over time, I realised that I am more than my past labels and emotions. I shed the diagnoses, discontinued medications, and banished suicidal thoughts and self-harm urges. I silenced shame and condemnation, turning to God and His Word to rediscover my true self and heal from within.

Embracing a Hopeful Future

As I graduated from Year 12, my principal spoke Jeremiah 29:11 over me:

"For I know the plans I have for you," declares the Lord, "plans to prosper you and not to harm you, plans to give you hope and a future."

This verse gained profound significance as I understood that God never intended suffering for me. His ultimate plan was for me to thrive. Despite the pain and overwhelming emotions, I found joy, peace, and ultimately, Him.

By Heleema Rawlings of KingdomCity Church; Western Australia

Permission has been given to share the following personal testimonies by Senior Pastor Michael Yeo of the Church of Praise, Johor Bahru. Malaysia:

https://youtube.com/playlist?list=PLl2l71p27lPDT-Qh_EMBNjpiiCsKkE0p4

Worship songs from Youtube Don Moen's Music

https://youtu.be/Guxfbxjx-nI?si=9Og8ujS744RKF4RV
https://www.youtube.com/watch?v=oAlXZ6aVf2U
https://youtu.be/7HDokgPLEQI?si=BbubuIPHsDXjFX4_
https://youtu.be/NjOGX5zT8KU?si=zdOA92cl4LvUYOYC

https://youtu.be/OMtoTdpFBJs?si=5USbTMUOh1vXngnShttps://youtu.be/OMtoTdpFBJs?si=5USbTMUOh1vXngnS

https://youtu.be/WZBOSfiH8Rk?si=mZ0pFbSfYI7Ksjcz

https://youtu.be/TmEYeZB8dDI?si=VmpYYbOBu2Bje8iZ

By Faith

https://youtu.be/WZBOSfiH8Rk?si=mZ0pFbSfYI7Ksjcz
https://youtu.be/TmEYeZB8dDI?si=VmpYYbOBu2Bje8iZ
https://youtu.be/I1GiZL60c80?si=iMmMNdbK0q19AlO
https://youtu.be/Rv9dZ0O0NCw?si=cFoP52euwGQf0nye
https://youtu.be/S2oGHaKpq-Q?si=sRrooWZwWv-U7nsn

Repeatable 30-Day Devotional Journey: Encountering God/Jesus and Growing in His Word

Introduction: Welcome to this 30-day devotional journey designed to help you encounter God and deepen your relationship with Jesus. Each day, we will explore a different topic and provide reflections, prayers, and Bible verses to guide you. May this journey strengthen your faith and empower you to grow in your relationship with God. Let's begin!

Day 1: Embracing God's Profound Love

Reflect on the depth of God's love for you
Read John 3, focusing on verses 16-17

Deeper understanding and experience of God's love are our focus point
Today, take a moment to contemplate the boundless depth of God's love for us. It's a love beyond comprehension, limitless, and unconditional. God's incredible act of sacrifice, as described in

"For God so loved the world that he gave his one and only Son, that whoever believes in him shall not perish but have eternal life...." - John 3:16–17

Pause for a moment; this love is beyond our understanding. Open your heart as you reflect on this verse.

Today, choose to embrace God's love. Let it transform your life, filling you with joy and peace. Make His love the cornerstone of your faith and relationship with Him.

In times of difficulty or uncertainty, remember that God's love is a constant wellspring of strength. Trust in His love, knowing that He is always with you, guiding you.

Commit to seeking a deeper understanding and experience of God's love. May it overflow in your life, touching and transforming everything you do.

Prayer: Heavenly Father, we thank you for your incredible love. Help us grasp its depth and fully embrace it in our lives. Grant us a deeper understanding and experience of your love. Fill us with your love, so it overflows in our relationships, thoughts, and actions. Guide us on this journey of faith, enabling us to walk in your love every day. In Jesus' name, Amen.

Day 2: Surrendering to God's Divine Plan

Explore the importance of surrendering to God's plans
Read Matthew 26, focusing on verse 39
Reflect on areas of your life where you need to surrender to God

Jesus demonstrates a profound act of relinquishment in the Garden of Gethsemane as an inspiring illustration of God's divine plans for our lives.

"Going a little farther, he fell with his face to the ground and prayed, 'My Father, if it is possible, may this cup be taken from me. Yet not as I will, but as you will.'" - Matthew 26:39

In this moment, Jesus, though human, surrendered His desires and fears to God's will. He trusted in God's perfect wisdom and love, understanding that divine plans exceed human comprehension.

Consider your life. Are there dreams, ambitions, or tightly held plans you need to surrender to God? Release control and invite God's guidance.

Surrendering isn't passive; it's an act of faith and trust, embracing God's extraordinary plan. It frees you from the burden of control, allowing God to lead you.

As you embark on this surrender journey, pray for a willing heart to align with God's will. Ask Him to reveal resistance within, seek His guidance for decisions, and ask for His strength to let go.

Prayer: Heavenly Father, today I surrender my life to Your will. Help me release my desires and trust in Your perfect timing and wisdom. Reveal areas of resistance and grant me strength to embrace Your plans. May I walk in obedience and faith, knowing Your ways are higher. In Jesus' name, Amen.

Day 3: Seeking God's Presence Daily

Discover the significance of seeking God's presence in your daily life
Read Psalm 105, focusing on verse 4
Set aside dedicated time to seek God's presence today

Today, let's explore the significance of seeking God's presence in our daily lives, guided by

"Look to the Lord and his strength; seek his face always." - Psalm 105:4

This verse encourages us to consistently seek God's presence, not just in times of need but in every aspect of life. Seeking God opens us to His strength, wisdom, and guidance.

Reflect on your life. Are there times you've neglected seeking God's presence, relying on your own strength? Let's commit to wholeheartedly seeking Him.

Dedicated time for seeking God's presence is essential. Whether through prayer, meditation, or reading His Word, prioritise this time to align with His will.

In His presence, find peace and refuge. Know you're not alone in struggles; God guides every step. Seek Him to transform your perspective, shifting focus from worldly concerns to eternal truths. His wisdom reveals His plans.

Seeking God's presence empowers you to reflect His love and grace. Be a vessel of His character and share His love.

Commit to daily seeking God's presence. Prioritise this time to commune with Him, surrender to His will, and experience His transformative power. Let His love motivate you to impact others.

Prayer: Heavenly Father, I seek Your presence daily. Help me prioritise this time, free from distractions. Fill me with strength, wisdom, and guidance.

Transform my perspective and use me to share Your love and grace. In Jesus' name, Amen.

Day 4: Growing in Faith

Learn about the process of growing in faith
Read Hebrews 11, focusing on verse 6
Reflect on ways you can actively grow in your faith

Nurturing Your Faith: Pleasing God, as it says in Hebrews 11:6, highlights the crucial role of faith in our relationship with God.

"Without faith, it is impossible to please God, because anyone who comes to him must believe that he exists and that he rewards those who earnestly seek him." - Hebrews 11:6

stating that without it, pleasing God is impossible, as it requires belief in His existence and promises.

Let's explore ways to actively nurture our faith. Faith is dynamic, requiring continuous care and attention.

One way to grow in faith is by immersing ourselves in God's Word. The Bible provides wisdom, guidance, and promises. By engaging with Scripture daily, we deepen our understanding of God's character and His purpose for us. Regular Bible reading and meditation transform our minds and strengthen our faith.

Prayer is another avenue for faith growth. It's not just about making requests; it's a means of connecting with God, seeking His will, and aligning our hearts with His. Dedicate daily time to pray, both in joy and adversity. Purposeful prayer invites God into our lives, reinforcing our faith.

Build a community of fellow believers. Fellowship with like-minded individuals offers support, encouragement, and accountability. Engage in worship, join a small group, or seek mentors for your faith journey. Together, you can nurture your faith and inspire one another toward deeper intimacy with God.

Embrace opportunities to step out in faith and trust God in new ways. Often, faith flourishes during challenges and beyond our comfort zones. Trust in God's provision, guidance, and empowerment as you obey His leading.

Growing in faith is a journey. Doubt, questions, and struggles may arise, but turn to God and lean on Him in those moments. Trust in His faithfulness, knowing He rewards those earnestly seeking Him.

Prayer: Heavenly Father, I desire to nurture my faith. Guide me to seek You actively through Scripture, prayer, and fellowship with fellow believers. Strengthen my faith and deepen my trust in You. Grant me the courage to step out in faith and embrace the opportunities You present. May my faith please You and bring glory to Your name. In Jesus' name, Amen.

Day 5: Trusting God's Timing

Reflect on the importance of trusting God's timing
Read Ecclesiastes 3, focusing on verse 1
Pray for patience and trust in God's perfect timing

As we come to the 5th day, let's delve into a meaningful teaching of God's timing. In Ecclesiastes 3:1, have we not been reminded time and again that there's a season and a time for everything:

"To everything there is a season and a time for every purpose under heaven" - Ecclesiastes 3:1

This verse emphasises that God is the master of time, with a perfect plan for each season in our lives. Trusting His timing brings us peace, contentment, and fulfilment.

Reflect on your life—are there areas where trusting God's timing is a challenge? Do impatience or the desire for quicker outcomes trouble you? Today, surrender those concerns to God and choose to trust His timing.

Trusting God's timing involves patience, faith, and surrender. It acknowledges His higher ways and eternal perspective. Even when we can't fathom His reasons, we trust that He works all things for our good.

In times of waiting and uncertainty, turn to prayer. Pray for patience and a deeper trust in His timing. Ask God to calm your anxious heart as you wait on Him.

Also, remember that God's timing often aligns with our growth and preparation. While waiting, He may refine us, strengthen our faith, or equip us for the future. Embrace the process, knowing God works within you during the wait.

Trusting God's timing involves surrendering your desires and agenda. It's an act of humility, acknowledging His superior plans. By yielding your timeline to Him, you open yourself to His best, even if it differs from your vision.

Today, choose to trust God's timing in all aspects of life. Surrender your desires, plans, and expectations. Pray for patience, faith, and deeper trust. Rest in the knowledge that God is working all things for your good, and His timing is always perfect.

Prayer: Heavenly Father, I surrender my desires and expectations to You. Grant me the strength to trust Your timing, even when it's challenging. Increase my patience and faith as I wait on You. Fill me with peace, knowing You're working everything for my good. May I find contentment and fulfilment in trusting Your perfect timing. In Jesus' name, Amen.

Day 6: Developing a Prayerful Life

Our prayer and relationship with God daily are called for ...

1 Thessalonians 5, focus on verses 16-18

In 1 Thessalonians 5:16-18, Day 6, we are urged to have a powerful prayerful life, as it has positive impacts on our connections with God.

"Rejoice always, pray continually, and give thanks in all circumstances; for this is God's will for you in Christ Jesus...."
- Thessalonians 5:16-18

These verses highlight a strong focus on our daily prayer lives. It transcends mere religious duty or seeking our needs; it's a means to commune with

God, seek His guidance, and express gratitude. Through it, we align our hearts with Him and experience His transformative work.

Take a moment to ponder your prayer life. Are there moments when you neglect communication with God or relegate prayer to an afterthought? Today, let's commit to setting aside dedicated time for prayer.

Allocate time today to pray and seek God's presence. Find a quiet space for intimate communion with Him. Pour out your heart, share your thoughts, and lay your burdens before Him. In prayer, we engage with our God, who listens and responds to our heartfelt cries.

Moreover, prayer fosters gratitude. When we thank God in all circumstances, we recognize His goodness, faithfulness, and provision. Even in adversity, we find reasons for gratitude, knowing God orchestrates all things for our benefit. Let gratitude accompany your prayer life, deepening trust and dependence on God.

Developing a prayerful life entails maintaining an ongoing conversation with God throughout the day. Pray continually, not just during designated times but in ordinary moments. Offer brief prayers of gratitude, guidance, and intercession as you go about your daily routines. This invites God into every facet of your life and acknowledges His presence in the mundane.

As we commit to cultivating a prayerful life, remember that prayer isn't a one-sided dialogue. It's a relationship-building exercise with our Heavenly Father. Take time to listen to His voice, discern His will, and be open to His guidance. Be attentive to His communication through His Word, others, and the gentle whispers of His Spirit.

Prayer: Heavenly Father, I yearn to nurture a prayerful life. Aid me in setting aside dedicated time for communion with You. Teach me to pray continuously, express gratitude in all circumstances, and attune my heart to Your voice. May my prayers deepen our relationship and impact the lives of others. In Jesus' name, Amen.

Day 7: Understanding God's Word

Reflect on the significance of studying and understanding God's Word
Read Psalm 119, focusing on verse 105
Commit to reading and studying the Bible regularly

"Your word is a lamp for my feet, a light on my path" - Psalm 119:105

demonstrates the power of God's Word, providing illumination and guidance for our lives and inspiring us to consider our relationship with the Bible.

Think for a moment to reflect on how to interact with the Bible. Have you been neglecting it? Let's commit to regular Bible study to gain a deeper understanding of God's truths.

Regularly reading and studying the Bible is vital for a strong faith foundation. Immersing ourselves in Scripture deepens our knowledge of God, His character, and His plans. Prioritise daily dedicated time for reading and meditation to shape your thoughts and actions.

Furthermore, studying the Bible helps us discern truth from falsehood in a world of conflicting messages. It serves as an unchanging anchor, offering timeless wisdom to navigate life's complexities.

Approach the Bible with humility and a teachable spirit, recognizing it as a living word from God. Invite the Holy Spirit to guide your study, reveal truths, and transform your heart and mind.

Studying God's Word deepens our relationship with Him. It's through Scripture that we encounter the living God, drawing closer and experiencing His love, grace, and presence.

Exploring God's Word reveals our identity and purpose. It reveals God's love, His redemptive plan, and our worth as His beloved children. This empowers us to live out our calling confidently and purposefully.

Today, commit to studying and understanding God's Word. Set aside daily time for reading and meditation. Approach it with an open heart to encounter God and gain wisdom, guidance, and a deeper understanding of yourself in Him.

Prayer: Heavenly Father, I commit to studying and understanding Your Word. Help me dedicate daily time to Scripture. Open my heart and mind to receive Your truths and be transformed by Your Word. Guide me through Your Spirit, deepening my relationship with You as I seek to understand Your Word. In Jesus' name, Amen.

Day 8: Experiencing God's Forgiveness

Contemplate the profound depth of God's forgiveness and the essential act of forgiving others.
Read Matthew 6, focusing on verses 14-15
Focus and seek a heart open to forgiveness.

In today's reflection on the transformative power of forgiveness, Matthew 6:14-15 underscores its pivotal role in our connection with God:

"If you forgive others when they wrong you, your heavenly Father will also forgive you. But if you refuse to forgive others, your Father will not forgive you."

These verses emphasise forgiveness's importance in our lives. Let's delve into the boundless and unconditional nature of God's forgiveness. Despite our sins, God's mercy is always accessible. Through Jesus Christ's sacrifice, God offers forgiveness, cleansing us from our sins and reconciling us with Him.

Consider the forgiveness you've received from God. Are there areas where accepting His forgiveness proves challenging? Open your heart to fully experience God's forgiveness, allowing it to revolutionise your life.

Encountering God's forgiveness compels us to extend the same grace to others. While not always easy, it is crucial for our well-being and growth. Clinging to grudges burdens us and impedes our spiritual progress.

When forgiving others, remember that it doesn't excuse the wrongs done to us. Instead, it's a conscious decision to release anger, resentment, and bitterness—a step toward healing.

Prayer serves as a potent tool to nurture a forgiving heart. Pray for a heart willing to forgive, even when it seems impossible. Seek God's assistance in releasing past hurts, allowing His love and grace to fill you. Trust in His ability to restore and heal as you choose forgiveness.

Forgiveness is an ongoing process, especially in cases of profound hurt or betrayal. Be patient with yourself and others on this journey. Lean on God's strength and seek support from trusted friends or mentors.

Prayer: Heavenly Father, grant me Your forgiveness and enable me to embrace it wholly. Soften my heart to forgive others as You have forgiven me. May I be a vessel of Your love, extending forgiveness to all who have wronged me. In Jesus' name, I pray. Amen.

Day 9: Cultivating a Grateful Heart: A Journey of Faith

Discover the power of gratitude in your relationship with God
Read 1 Thessalonians 5, focusing on verse 18
Reflect on the blessings in your life and express gratitude to God

In our faith journey, nurturing a grateful heart is profoundly transformative. Gratitude draws us closer to God, enriches our relationship with Him, and positively impacts humanity. Let's explore its significance.

"Give thanks in all circumstances; for this is God's will for you in Christ Jesus." - 1 Thessalonians 5:18

True gratitude thrives when we choose to be thankful, even amid challenges.

Reflect on life's blessings, from shelter and food to love and relationships. Cultivating a grateful heart allows us to appreciate life's meaningful details.

Gratitude deepens our connection with God. It acknowledges His sovereignty and love, drawing us closer to Him. It fosters trust, love, and reverence in our relationship.

Gratitude's impact extends beyond personal growth. It's contagious, making us more compassionate and considerate. This positivity enriches our interactions, bridging divides and fostering unity.

Imagine a world where everyone embraces gratitude, appreciates blessings, and acknowledges others' contributions. Such a world would overflow with love, empathy, and joy.

Prayer: Heavenly Father, I'm grateful for life's blessings, big and small. Help me embrace gratitude in all circumstances. Teach me to appreciate others, be a source of love and kindness, and make a positive difference in the world. Amen

Day 10: Spreading God's Love

Explore the significance of sharing God's love with others
Read Matthew 28, focusing on verses 19-20
Identify opportunities to show God's love to those around you

Today, we explore the profound theme of sharing God's love as we continue our faith journey. This mission is pivotal, impacting individual lives and shaping humanity.

Matthew 28:19-20 echoes Jesus' commission to His disciples:

"Go therefore and make disciples of all the nations, baptizing them in the name of the Father and of the Son and of the Holy Spirit, teaching them to observe all things that I have commanded you; and lo, I am with you always, even to the end of the age. Amen."

This emphasises actively sharing God's love and message, transcending boundaries.

Sharing God's love involves proclaiming the Gospel and embodying Christ's love through our actions. Being compassionate, kind, and understanding is vital. We become living testimonies of God's grace and mercy.

Opportunities to demonstrate God's love abound in our daily lives. Listening to a friend in need, offering assistance, or providing encouragement can profoundly impact others, spreading hope and healing.

Engaging in community service and supporting marginalised individuals are tangible ways to show God's love. Volunteering, aiding charitable organisations, or participating in outreach programs make a significant difference.

Sharing God's love also entails embracing diversity, treating all with respect and dignity, and fostering unity and harmony. Our love should mirror God's boundless love.

As we heed the call to share God's love, we become agents of transformation. Each act, no matter how small, has a ripple effect, touching countless lives. By living out the Great Commission, we contribute to a world where love, compassion, and understanding prevail, profoundly impacting humanity.

Prayer: Heavenly Father, guide me to be a vessel of your love. Help me show kindness, compassion, and inclusivity. May my actions reflect your love, bring hope, and contribute to spreading your message of grace and salvation. Amen.

Day 11: Conquering Fear and Anxiety

Reflect on God's promise to be with you and provide peace
Read Isaiah 41, focusing on verse 10
Pray for the strength to overcome fear and anxiety

In our faith journey, we often face fear and anxiety. However, we find reassurance and strength in God's promise to be with us and grant us peace amidst life's challenges. Isaiah 41:10 offers this comforting message.

God assures us in

"Do not fear, for I am with you; do not be dismayed, for I am your God. I will strengthen you, help you, and uphold you with my righteous right hand." - Isaiah 41:10

These words remind us that we're not alone; God provides strength and guidance.

Fear and anxiety often stem from uncertainty about the future or life's challenges. Yet, we serve a God who holds the universe and cares deeply for us. He knows our struggles and promises unwavering love and protection.

Through prayer, we seek strength to conquer fear and anxiety, pouring out our concerns to God. Surrendering these burdens opens us to His transcendent peace, guarding our hearts and minds in life's storms.

Prayer: Heavenly Father, in moments of fear and anxiety, I turn to You. Thank you for Your promise to be with me and provide peace. Strengthen me with Your unwavering love and help me overcome my fears. I trust in Your righteous right hand to uphold me. Grant me the peace that surpasses all understanding as I surrender my worries to You. Amen.

Day 12: Strengthening Faith through Relationships

Discover the importance of healthy relationships in your faith journey
Read Proverbs 27, focusing on verse 17
Reflect on ways to strengthen your relationships with others

In our faith journey, our relationship with God takes precedence as the bedrock of spiritual growth. However, it's vital to acknowledge the profound influence of healthy human connections on our spiritual development.

Our interactions with others should be like the sharpening of iron:

"As iron sharpens iron, so one person sharpens another."
Proverbs 27:17

Just as iron gains sharpness by rubbing against another, our character, faith, and understanding mature through meaningful interactions with fellow believers.

Meaningful, healthy relationships offer companionship, accountability, and growth prospects. They enable us to encounter God's love, grace, and compassion through the individuals He places in our lives. By fostering positive relationships, we not only fortify our faith but also cultivate a supportive, uplifting environment for others.

Here are strategies to enrich your relationships:

Be intentional: Actively connect with others, showing genuine interest in their life journeys.

Practise active listening: Engage empathetically when others express their thoughts and feelings.

Extend Grace and Forgiveness: Promote an environment of reconciliation and growth by offering grace and forgiveness during challenges.

Serve One Another: Strengthen bonds through acts of kindness and selflessness.

Pray for One Another: Unite hearts in prayer, inviting God's presence into your relationships.

By investing in fortifying these relationships, we contribute to a community that mirrors Christ's love. Our lives become testimonials of His transformative power, drawing others closer to Him through bonds of fellowship and love.

Prayer: Heavenly Father, we thank you for the gift of relationships and their profound impact on our faith journey. Guide us in nurturing healthy, meaningful connections that sharpen and uplift one another in our walk with you. Endow us with wisdom, grace, and a servant's heart. May our relationships radiate your love and glorify Your name. Amen.

Day 13: Discovering Unshakable Hope in Christ

Reflect on the hope that comes from your relationship with Jesus
Read Romans 15, focusing on verse 13
Pray for an unwavering hope in Christ during challenging times

Amid life's trials and uncertainties, our connection with Jesus serves as an unswerving wellspring of hope. He anchors our souls, offering solace, fortitude, and assurance. Let's ponder the hope that stems from our knowledge of Him and reflect on Romans 15:13 as a reminder of the abundant hope we possess in Christ.

Life's tribulations can leave us feeling overwhelmed, anxious, or uncertain about the future. In these moments, we can turn to Jesus, our unwavering hope. Our hope in Christ isn't tethered to transient circumstances but is rooted in His immutable character and promises.

"May the God of hope fill you with all joy and peace as you trust in him so that you may overflow with hope by the power of the Holy Spirit." - Romans 15:13

This verse beautifully encapsulates the essence of hope in Christ. It underscores that God is the source of hope. As we entrust ourselves to Him, He infuses us with joy, peace, and overflowing hope through the Holy Spirit's work.

Our hope in Christ allows us to persevere with courage in the face of adversity, knowing He reigns. We find peace in His presence, strength in His Word, and certainty in His love. Our hope is anchored in His unchanging nature; He is the same yesterday, today and forever more.

Through our hope in Christ, we become beacons of light and agents of hope for those around us. Our lives bear witness to the transformational power of faith, inspiring others to seek the hope only Jesus provides. As we radiate His hope, we uplift and encourage those enduring difficult times, pointing them toward the ultimate wellspring of enduring hope and serenity.

Prayer: Heavenly Father, we thank you for the hope we uncover in Christ. During trying times, we seek You as our sanctuary and anchor. As we entrust ourselves to You, fill us with joy, peace, and overflowing hope through the Holy Spirit's power.

Help us cling to this unshakeable hope in Christ, even when circumstances appear uncertain. May our lives testify to Your faithfulness and grace, impacting those around us with the hope found solely in You. Amen.

Day 14: The Profound Impact of Humility in Our Walk with God

Explore the significance of humility in your relationship with God
Read Philippians 2, focusing on verses 3-4
Reflect on areas in your life where you can grow in humility

Humility is a profound virtue in our connection with God. It opens our hearts to His presence, recognizing His sovereignty and grace. Let's delve into the impact of humility on encountering God, reflect on Philippians 2:3-4, and explore areas where we can cultivate more humility.

The trait of humility is completely different from pride, which can form obstacles between us and God. By having a humble approach towards God, we confess that we depend on Him and recognize that He is the root of all knowledge, power, and morality. This type of modest outlook permits us to accept God's affection and direction by giving up our self-sufficiency and preferring His wishes rather than our own.

Philippians 2:3-4 provides guidance

"Do nothing out of selfish ambition or vain conceit. Rather, in humility, value others above yourselves, not looking to your own interests but each of you to the interests of others."

This Scripture encourages us to focus on others with genuine care and empathy, setting aside selfish desires. When we practise humility in our interactions, we create an atmosphere of love, unity, and understanding.

Take a moment to reflect on areas where you can nurture humility. This self-examination may reveal moments when pride creeps in, such as seeking recognition, making comparisons, or hesitating to serve those we consider less important. Identifying these areas allows us to actively cultivate a humble heart, aligning with Christ's example.

Encountering God with humility transforms us in His presence. Our hearts become receptive to His guidance, deepening our intimacy with our Heavenly Father. As we continue our faith journey, let's remember the significance of humility and its influence on our relationship with God and humanity.

Prayer: Heavenly Father, we thank you for Jesus' example of humility. Guide us as we grow in humility, recognizing our dependence on You and esteeming others above ourselves. Reveal areas where pride hinders our relationships with You and others.

May our encounters with You be marked by humble hearts, open to your wisdom and grace. Use us as vessels of your love and compassion, impacting humanity to reflect your character. Amen.

Day 15: Experiencing God's Presence in Worship

Discover the role of worship in your relationship with God
Read Psalm 100, focusing on verse 2
Engage in meaningful worship today and express your love to God

Worship holds a crucial role in our connection with God. It's a powerful means to draw near to Him, encounter His presence, and express our love and adoration. Let's explore the importance of worship and contemplate Psalm 100:2 as we engage in meaningful worship today, offering our hearts and voices to God.

Worship isn't a mere ritual or routine; it's a heartfelt response to God's greatness and goodness.

Psalm 100:2 beautifully captures this essence:

"Worship the Lord with gladness; come before him with joyful songs."

When we approach God with gladness and joy, raising our voices in praise, our hearts align with His, and we experience His presence in a profound way.

In worship, we fix our attention on God, leaving behind distractions and worldly concerns. It's a time of surrender, where we release our burdens and find rest in His presence. Through worship, we acknowledge His sovereignty and worthiness, recognizing that He alone deserves our praise and devotion.

Meaningful worship deepens our relationship with God. We open our hearts, allowing His love and grace to transform us from within. Worship reminds us of His faithfulness and goodness, strengthening our faith and trust in Him.

The impact of worship goes beyond our individual encounters with God. When we join others in corporate worship, we become part of a community united in adoration. Our collective voices rise like a symphony of praise, reflecting the diversity and beauty of humanity's worship of its Creator.

By expressing our love for God through worship, we influence the world around us. Our worship becomes a testament to God's love, drawing others to seek Him and encounter His presence. Through our worship, we inspire hope, provide healing, and share the message of God's grace with those who may not yet know Him.

So, let's engage in worship today with hearts full of gladness and joy. May our songs and prayers be offerings of love to the One who loves us immeasurably. In worship, may we encounter God's presence and be transformed by His unwavering love.

Prayer: Heavenly Father, we thank you for the gift of worship, where we can draw near to you and experience your presence. Today, we come before you with gladness and joy, lifting our voices in praise and adoration.

As we worship You, may our hearts be transformed by Your love and grace. Use our worship to impact others, reflecting your goodness and drawing them closer to You. Amen.

Day 16: Serving Others with Love Discover Opportunities to Serve Others with Love and Compassion

Identify ways we can serve others with love and compassion
Exploring Acts of Love and Service Understanding the Significance of Serving in Jesus' Name
Read Mark 10, focusing on verse 45

In our modern, fast-paced world, where self-interest often takes precedence, the act of serving others carries immense spiritual importance. Jesus, the epitome of love and compassion, exemplified the significance of selfless service during His earthly tenure. Let's delve into the profound message conveyed in Mark 10:45 and learn how we can embody Jesus' heart of service in our lives.

"For even the Son of Man did not come to be served, but to serve, and to give his life as a ransom for many." - Mark 10:45

This scripture encapsulates the core of Jesus' earthly mission. He didn't seek admiration or praise; instead, He humbly served others with boundless love and compassion. In our daily lives, this means actively seeking opportunities to assist and uplift others, not for personal recognition but to mirror the love of Christ.

Serving others in the name of Jesus is a tangible expression of our faith. It transcends mere assistance; it embodies Jesus' teachings through our actions. When we serve with love and compassion, we become channels of God's grace, reflecting His unconditional love for those around us. Through serving, we actively partake in God's divine plan, spreading kindness and instilling hope in a world often mired in despair.

Reflect upon the unique gifts and talents bestowed upon you by God. Ponder how these abilities can be utilised to serve others. It might entail volunteering at a local shelter, mentoring a struggling friend, supporting a charitable cause, or simply offering a listening ear to someone in need. Acts of service, regardless of their scale, possess the power to profoundly impact lives and glorify God.

Prayer: Heavenly Father, We express gratitude for the exemplary life of Your Son, Jesus Christ, who came not to be served but to serve. Open our eyes to the people who need You. Strengthen our hearts, O Lord, and lead us in our endeavours to reflect Your love through our actions. May our service stand as a testimony to Your grace and bring honour to Your name. In Jesus' name, we pray. Amen.

As we meditate on Mark 10:45, let's wholeheartedly embrace the call to serve others with love and compassion. Through our actions, we not only fulfil God's commandment but also reflect the heart of Jesus to a world thirsting for His love. Let our deeds serve as beacons of hope, illuminating every corner of our lives with the radiant light of Christ.

Day 17: Finding Strength in Weakness

Reflect on God's power and strength in your moments of weakness
Read 2 Corinthians 12, focusing on verse 9
Pray for God's strength to be made perfect in our weakness

Today, let's ponder the significance of humility in finding strength during our weakest moments, recognizing that it's precisely in these times that we can witness the full extent of God's power and might. Often, our human nature pushes us to rely on our own abilities. However, when we acknowledge our vulnerabilities and yield to God, we discover genuine strength.

In 2 Corinthians 12:9, the apostle Paul shares a powerful insight:

"But he said to me, 'My grace is sufficient for you, for my power is made perfect in weakness.' Therefore, I will boast all the more gladly about my weaknesses, so that Christ's power may rest on me."

These words emphasise that true victory doesn't stem from our own strength but from God's divine power working through us.

When we humbly admit our limitations, we create space for God's strength to shine through our weaknesses. In those moments of surrender, we experience the grace and power of God at work within us. Our weaknesses don't limit God; rather, He seizes them as opportunities to showcase His power and glorify His name.

Take a moment to reflect on your own weaknesses and areas where you might feel inadequate. Instead of being disheartened by them, invite God into those very spaces. Ask Him to infuse you with His strength, surrendering your weaknesses to His care. Trust that His power will radiate brilliantly through your moments of weakness.

Prayer: Dear Heavenly Father, We thank you for the profound reminder that Your grace is more than enough for us, and Your power is most fully realised in our weaknesses. Grant us the ability to embrace our vulnerabilities and place them in Your loving hands. Fill us with Your unwavering strength, enabling us to lean on You in every facet of our lives. May Your magnificent power shine through us, bringing honour to Your name. We pray this in Jesus' name. Amen.

Day 18: Pursuing Holiness

Reflect on the call to live a holy life for God

Read 1 Peter 1, focusing on verses 15-16
Identify areas in your life where you can pursue holiness

Today, let us reflect on the impact of humility in pursuing holiness. As followers of Christ, we are called to live a life that is set apart for God and marked by righteousness and purity. Our pursuit of holiness is not something we do in our strength; it is a response to God's call and a surrender to His transforming work in our lives.

"But just as he who called you is holy, so be holy in all you do; for it is written: 'Be holy, because I am holy.'" - 1 Peter 1:15-16

These verses remind us that God, who is holy, has called us to reflect His holiness in everything we do. Pursuing holiness is not about earning our salvation; it is a response to the grace and love that God has shown us.

Humility plays a crucial role in our pursuit of holiness. It is through humility that we recognize our need for God's guidance and transformation in our lives. We acknowledge that we cannot achieve holiness on our own, but we depend on God's grace and the power of the Holy Spirit to work in us.

Take a moment to reflect on your own life. In what areas can you pursue holiness? It may be in your thoughts, words, actions, or relationships. Ask God to reveal any areas where you need to grow in holiness and humility. Surrender those areas to Him and seek His guidance and strength to live a life that honours Him.

Prayer : Dear Heavenly Father, thank you for calling us to a life of holiness. Help us to pursue holiness with humility, knowing that it is only through Your grace and power that we can grow in righteousness. Show us any areas in our lives where we need to grow in holiness and give us the strength to surrender those areas to You. May our pursuit of holiness bring glory to Your name and draw others closer to You. In Jesus' name, we pray. Amen.

Day 19: Building a Christ-Centred Family

Explore the importance of nurturing a Christ-centred family
Read Joshua 24, focusing on verse 15
Pray for your family's faith to be strengthened and centred on Jesus

Today, let's delve into the crucial significance of nurturing a Christ-centred family amidst the distractions and competing priorities of the world. In the words of Joshua 24:15, he powerfully declares to the Israelites:

"And if it seems evil to you to serve the Lord, choose for yourselves this day whom you will serve, whether the gods which your fathers served that were on the other side of the River, or the gods of the Amorites, in whose land you dwell. But as for me and my house, we will serve the Lord."

Joshua recognized the profound importance of guiding his family in the ways of the Lord, deliberately prioritising God in their lives.

To build a Christ-centred family, it begins with our personal commitment to follow Jesus. As our faith deepens, we can impart this faith to our family through our words, actions, and attitudes. Within our homes, we can create an atmosphere characterised by love, grace, and forgiveness, mirroring Christ's nature.

Reflect on your family. How can you nurture a Christ-centred environment within it? It might involve setting aside time for family devotionals, praying together, attending church collectively, or engaging in faith discussions. Ponder how you can consciously prioritise Jesus in your family's daily life.

Prayer: Heavenly Father, We are grateful for the gift of family. Strengthen our family's faith and guide us in building a Christ-centred home. May our words, actions, and attitudes echo Your love and grace. Lead us in creating an environment where faith in Jesus flourishes. Assist us in making intentional choices that place You at the centre of our family life. In Jesus' name, we pray. Amen.

As you continue this journey of fostering a Christ-centred family, remember that it's a gradual process. Be patient and steadfast in your efforts, trusting that God will honour your endeavours.

Day 20: Seeking Wisdom from God

Reflect on the value of seeking God's wisdom in decision-making
Read James 1, focusing on verse 5
Seek God's wisdom in a specific decision you are facing

In our faith journey, seeking God's wisdom in decision-making holds immense importance, especially during pivotal moments. This practice showcases our reliance on His guidance and reveals our humility before our all-knowing Creator. Let's delve into the profound significance of seeking God's wisdom and ponder James 1:5 as we seek His guidance in specific decisions.

James 1:5 reassures us with these words:

"If any of you lacks wisdom, you should ask God, who gives generously to all without finding fault, and it will be given to you."

This promise underscores God's eagerness to provide wisdom to those earnestly seeking Him. We turn to the ultimate source of wisdom and knowledge rather than merely depending on our constrained comprehension.

Asking God for wisdom is a sign of confidence, a recognition that He knows what's best for us even when we don't fully understand the effects of our choices. By giving Him control over our plans, we make ourselves more receptive to His heavenly guidance.

External influences, such as societal expectations or personal ambitions, often cloud our judgement in decision-making. Seeking God's wisdom helps us sift through these distractions, aligning our hearts with His will. His wisdom brings clarity and peace amid uncertainty.

As you contemplate a specific decision, earnestly seek God's wisdom through prayer and His Word. Be receptive to His guidance, even if it leads you in a different direction. Trust that His plans always work for your ultimate good.

By seeking God's wisdom, we not only make wiser decisions but also positively impact those around us. Following His guidance transforms us into vessels of His wisdom and grace, illuminating the world with His light.

Prayer: Almighty Father, I come before You humbly, seeking Your wisdom in the decision ahead of me. I trust in your guidance, knowing you understand what's best. As I seek Your wisdom through prayer and Your Word, reveal my path. Align my desires with your will, giving me the courage to follow your lead, even in challenging times. Thank you for your generous provision of wisdom. May my choices bring glory to your name and positively influence others. Amen.

Day 21: Experiencing God's Peace

Discover the peace that surpasses all understanding through Christ
Read Philippians 4, focusing on verse 7
Pray for God's peace to fill your heart and mind today

Discovering a peace that defies understanding is possible through Christ. The peace mentioned in Philippians 4:7, is profound. It is expressed independently of our circumstances and springs from the faith and trust we have in our Heavenly Father.

"And the peace of God, which transcends all understanding, will guard your hearts and your minds in Christ Jesus." - Philippians 4:7

This verse emphasises that God's peace surpasses anything the world can offer, providing deep tranquillity and assurance even amid life's uncertainties.

In the presence of God's peace, fear, anxiety, and worry dissipate. We find comfort in the understanding that our Heavenly Father is in control, crafting a perfect plan for our lives. This peace doesn't rely on our abilities or circumstances; it is grounded in the unchanging character of God.

Encountering this divine peace transforms our approach to life. We learn to release our worries, trusting that God will turn everything around for our good. This peace acts as a shield, protecting our hearts and minds from being overwhelmed by the world's challenges and enabling us to confront each day with confidence and hope.

In moments of distress, we can actively seek God's peace through prayer. By entrusting our concerns to Him, we invite His peace to flood our hearts and minds. Through prayer, we acknowledge our dependence on Him, resting our trust in His unwavering love and wisdom.

Prayer: Heavenly Father, I pray for Your peace to fill my heart and mind today. In life's uncertainties, help me to trust in Your plan and provision. Shield me from fear and anxiety, and grant me the peace that transcends understanding. May Your peace reshape how I approach challenges and uncertainties. Thank you for being my wellspring of strength and peace. In Jesus' name, Amen.

Day 22: Walking in God's Light

Reflect on the call to walk in God's light and live a righteous life
Read 1 John 1, focusing on verse 7
Examine areas of your life where you can align with God's light

Reflecting on the call to walk in God's light and live a righteous life is essential for followers of Christ. This means aligning our lives with God's truth and allowing His guidance to illuminate our path. Let's contemplate this call and meditate on 1 John 1:7, focusing on areas in our lives where we can align ourselves with His light.

1 John 1:7 emphasises,

"But if we walk in the light, as he is in the light, we have fellowship with one another, and the blood of Jesus, his Son, purifies us from all sin."

Walking in God's light deepens our fellowship with Him and fellow believers. This intimate communion allows the cleansing and transforming power of Jesus' blood to wash away our sins, setting us on a righteous path.

Walking in God's light demands humility, surrendering our will to His and seeking His guidance in every aspect of our lives. It means acknowledging our need for His wisdom and strength to live righteously. This journey involves regular self-examination, allowing God's light to reveal any hidden darkness or sin requiring His forgiveness and healing.

Consider areas in your life where alignment with God's light is necessary. Are there behavioral patterns or attitudes that need surrendering? Is there a need for forgiveness, either seeking it or extending it to others? Invite the Holy Spirit to reveal areas needing realignment with God's truth.

As we walk in God's light and live righteously, our actions influence those around us. Our humility and obedience serve as a testament to God's transformative work, inspiring others to seek His light. Through our words and deeds, we can bring hope and encouragement, guiding others toward the true source of light and life—Jesus Christ.

Prayer: Heavenly Father, thank you for calling us to walk in Your light and live righteously. As I examine my heart and actions, I reveal areas needing realignment with Your truth and forgiveness. Grant me the humility to surrender my will to Yours and seek Your guidance in all I do. May my life testify to Your transforming power, offering hope and encouragement to others. Amen.

Day 23: Growing in Patience

Explore the significance of patience in your faith journey
Read Romans 12, focusing on verse 12
Pray for patience in waiting on God's timing and plans

Let's delve into the vital role of patience in our faith journey. Patience isn't merely a virtue; it's a fundamental quality as we navigate life's trials. Through patience, we learn to place our trust in God's timing and divine plans, even when uncertainty and anxiety cast shadows over us.

Romans 12:12 provides our guiding light:

"Be joyful in hope, patient in affliction, faithful in prayer."

These words emphasise the significance of patience in our connection with God. Patience equips us to endure challenging seasons, firmly believing that God is at work, even when the outcome remains unclear. It's through patience that our faith undergoes testing and refinement, and we draw closer to God.

Patience isn't synonymous with passive waiting; it demands active trust in God's timing and intricate plans. It necessitates surrendering our desires and aligning ourselves with His flawless will. Patience nurtures perseverance, resilience, and a profound reliance on God.

Take a moment to ponder your own faith journey. Where do you need to cultivate patience? Are there situations where waiting on God's timing feels daunting? Surrender those areas to God and seek His guidance in developing patience and trust.

Prayer: Heavenly Father, bestow upon us the gift of patience as we walk this journey with You. Grant us the ability to trust Your timing and plans, especially in moments of anxiety and uncertainty. Teach us to find joy in hope, to endure patiently in adversity, and to remain steadfast in prayer. Strengthen us when we struggle to wait on Your timing. May our lives bear witness to the patience and trust we place in You, bringing glory to Your name. In Jesus' name, we pray. Amen.

Throughout your day, remember to nurture patience in all aspects of life. Trust in God's timing and plans, knowing that He is faithful and will unfailingly fulfill His promises. Let your patience serve as a testament to your unwavering faith in Him.

Day 24: Loving Your Neighbour

Reflect on the commandment to love your neighbour as yourself
Read Matthew 22, focusing on verse 39
Identify practical ways to demonstrate love to your neighbours

Today, let's delve into the profound directive of loving our neighbors as we love ourselves. In a world often marked by division and strife, it has become crucial for us to embody Christ's love and generously extend it to those around us. Jesus doesn't simply encourage us to speak of love; He challenges us to manifest it through tangible actions.

"You shall love your neighbour as yourself." - Matthew 22:39

The verse we're focusing on, Matthew 22:39, underscores the significance of treating others with love, kindness, and respect. Matthew is effectively teaching us how to interact with our fellow human beings, acknowledging their intrinsic worth as bearers of God's image.

As we ponder this divine guidance, let's actively brainstorm practical ways to demonstrate love for our neighbours. It could be as simple as extending a helping hand, lending a compassionate ear, or infusing kindness into our everyday interactions.

Take a moment to consider whether there are specific individuals or communities you can support and uplift. Through prayer, seek guidance to identify tangible ways to exhibit God's love. Empower yourself to engage in acts of service and compassion.

Throughout your day, keep in mind the paramount importance of loving your neighbours. Actively seek opportunities to extend love, compassion, and unwavering support to those in your immediate vicinity. Let our actions speak louder than words; let Christ's love shine through our actions; and bring forth hope and healing to the desperate..

Prayer: Heavenly Father, we stand before You in humility and adoration, thanking You for the crucial command to love our neighbours as ourselves. Grant us the strength to manifest this love through our actions. Illuminate practical ways for us to exhibit love to those around us. Open our hearts to perceive the needs of others and infuse in us the courage to respond with unwavering compassion and kindness. May our love mirror Yours and bring immense glory to Your holy name. In Jesus' name, we pray. Amen.

Day 25: Trusting God in Times of Trials

Discover the faithfulness of God in times of trials and difficulties
Read Psalm 46, focusing on verses 1-2
Pray for trust and reliance on God in the midst of challenges

In our life journey, we encounter a multitude of trials and tribulations, spanning in all directions, from financial hardship to health complications to difficulties in our relationships. You may say adversity is an inherent part of experience, knocking at different stages of our lives. In these very trying moments, we must maintain constant focus and cling to the unwavering belief that God is perpetually on our side, on which we can depend.

Let us direct our focus to Psalm 46:1-2 and allow the profound truth within these verses to resonate deeply within our hearts:

"God is our refuge and strength, an ever-present help in trouble. Therefore, we will not fear, though the earth give way and the mountains fall into the heart of the sea."

These words stand as a poignant reminder that even when our world appears to crumble, God remains our sanctuary and the wellspring of our strength. His perpetual assistance serves as a guiding light, leading us through the trials we encounter. By entrusting our faith in Him, we can confront life's uncertainties without succumbing to fear.

Let us take a moment to offer a heartfelt prayer, seeking profound trust and reliance on God amidst our challenges.

Prayer: Heavenly Father, we humbly come before You with gratitude for being our refuge and strength during times of trial. We place our complete trust in You, acknowledging that our lives rest securely in Your hands. Strengthen us, O Lord, to confront challenges with unwavering confidence, always mindful of Your unwavering faithfulness. Grant us the wisdom to discern Your will and the grace to surrender our plans to You. We depend wholeheartedly on Your enduring love to carry us through. In the name of Jesus, we fervently pray. Amen.

Day 26: Receiving God's Grace

Reflect on the abundant grace that God freely offers
Read Ephesians 2, focusing on verses 8-9
Meditate on the significance of God's grace in your life

Let's delve into the profound gift of God's grace, a gift freely given to us despite our flaws and imperfections. Through His grace, we discover salvation and nurture a life-giving relationship with Him. Consider the magnitude of God's grace for a moment, and then read Ephesians 2:8-9 to fully grasp its significance.

Ephesians 2:8-9 reminds us, "For it is by grace you have been saved, through faith—and this is not from yourselves; it is the gift of God—not by works, so that no one can boast."

This verse emphasises that our redemption is the consequence of God's unearned favour and kindness, not our own efforts. It underlines His boundless love and mercy, diving into our brokenness and giving forgiveness and new life in Christ.

As we contemplate the profound significance of God's grace, let's humbly acknowledge our need for it. Embracing the truth that His grace is freely given to all who believe in and receive Jesus Christ as their Savior, we recognize that we cannot save ourselves; our righteousness comes solely through Christ. God's grace profoundly impacts us, bringing transformation and liberating us from the chains of sin, empowering us to live a life that honors Him.

In receiving His grace, we are called to extend grace to others, demonstrating His love and compassion to a world in need.

Prayer: Heavenly Father, we are profoundly grateful for Your abundant grace that saves and liberates us. We humbly receive this precious gift, fully aware that we cannot earn it. Help us grasp the immense significance of Your grace in our lives, bringing transformation and shaping us to resemble Jesus. As we bask in Your grace, empower us to extend the same love and compassion to others, impacting humanity and sharing Your salvation. Amen.

Day 27: Pursuing Unity in the Body of Christ

Explore the importance of unity among believers in the Church
Read Romans 12, focusing on verses 4-5
Reflect on ways you can contribute to unity in your church community

Today, let's explore seeking unity in the body of Christ. According to Paul in Romans 12:4-5, the body of Christ is made up of many parts, but all form one body. Unity among believers is essential for the church to function effectively. Just as a body needs all its parts working together, the church needs diverse individuals with unique gifts and roles, held together by unity.

To contribute to unity in our church communities, we must value the uniqueness of each member. We should seek to understand and appreciate different gifts, perspectives, and experiences. Prioritising others above ourselves and practicing humility and love builds connections and eliminates divisions. Healthy relationships, forgiveness, and reconciliation are crucial for nurturing unity.

Prayer plays a vital role in uniting believers. As we pray for one another, our hearts align with the Lord's desire for unity. Prayer allows us to set aside personal agendas and invite the Holy Spirit to guide and shape us into a united body.

In conclusion, pursuing unity in the body of Christ requires intentional effort. Let's remember that unity is a reflection of God's desire for His church. Together, let's actively work towards unity, embodying the love and grace of Christ that binds us together.

Prayer: Heavenly Father, we acknowledge the significance of unity in the body of Christ. Help us embrace the uniqueness of each member, creating bridges of love and understanding. Guide us in practising humility and selflessness. Pour out Your Spirit upon us, enabling us to put aside differences, forgive, and seek reconciliation. We thank You for the privilege of being part of Your church, and we pray for the manifestation of unity that brings glory to Your name. Amen.

Day 28: Sharing Your Faith with Boldness

Reflect on the call to share your faith with confidence and boldness
Read Acts 4, focusing on verse 31
Pray for opportunities and courage to share your faith

Today, let's consider the significance of sharing our faith with confidence and boldness, as exemplified in Acts 4:31.

"After they prayed, the place where they were meeting was shaken. And they were all filled with the Holy Spirit and spoke the word of God boldly."

The early disciples faced opposition and challenges, yet they prayed fervently for courage. Their prayer was answered and they were filled with the Holy Spirit, enabling them to proclaim God's word boldly.

Sharing our faith isn't always easy. Doubts, fear of rejection, or uncertainty about how others may react can hold us back. But God calls us to share His love and truth with the world, standing firm in our convictions.

Consider the times when you've held back from sharing your faith. What held you back? Was it fear, uncertainty, or a concern for how others might perceive you? Reflect on how God's Spirit can empower you to overcome these barriers. We're reminded that boldness in sharing our faith doesn't mean arrogance or forcefulness. It's about speaking truth with love, guided by the conviction of the Holy Spirit. Take a moment to reflect on your experiences sharing your faith. Recall times when you've felt empowered by the Spirit to speak boldly about God's love and truth. Consider the impact those moments had on others and on your own faith journey. As you go through your day, ask God for opportunities to share your faith and the courage to embrace those opportunities. Pray for the guidance of the Holy Spirit to speak with wisdom, love, and boldness, touching hearts and bringing others closer to God.

Prayer: Heavenly Father, grant me the courage to share my faith boldly. Open doors for conversations and moments where I can express Your love and truth to those around me. Fill me with Your Holy Spirit, guiding my words and actions. May I reflect Your love in all that I do. In Jesus' name, Amen.

May you find strength in God's Spirit as you step forward in faith, sharing His love and truth with boldness and compassion.

Prayer: Heavenly Father, we acknowledge the paramount importance of unity within the body of Christ. Help us embrace the uniqueness of each member, building bridges of love and understanding. Guide us in practicing humility and selflessness. Pour out Your Spirit upon us, enabling us to set aside differences, forgive, and seek reconciliation. We are grateful for the privilege of being part of Your church, and we earnestly pray for the manifestation of unity that brings glory to Your name. Amen.

Day 29: Seeking God's Guidance

Discover the importance of seeking God's guidance in decision-making
Read Proverbs 3, focusing on verses 5-6
Pray for wisdom and discernment in your choices

In our 29th devotion, let's delve into the significance of seeking God's guidance when making decisions, a practice essential to our faith journey. This approach aligns our choices with God's divine will, leading to wisdom and inner peace.

Let's begin by meditating on Proverbs 3:5-6:

"Trust in the LORD with all your heart and lean not on your own understanding; in all your ways submit to him, and he will make your paths straight."

This passage urges us to wholeheartedly trust the Lord and let go of our dependence on human reasoning. It invites us to surrender our decisions to Him, acknowledging His sovereignty and perfect wisdom.

When we actively seek God's guidance, we invite Him into every aspect of our lives, recognising that He knows what is best for us. This practice helps us avoid impulsive or self-centred choices, aligning us with His divine plans.

In the face of various decisions and challenges, it's crucial to pray for wisdom and discernment.

James 1:5 reminds us,

"If any of you lack wisdom, you should ask God, who gives generously... and it will be given to you."

God is eager to bestow His wisdom, but we must actively seek it through prayer.

As we continue our faith journey, let's always remember the importance of seeking God's guidance in our decision-making process. Trust in Him wholeheartedly, pray fervently for wisdom, and willingly surrender our choices to His perfect will. May God abundantly bless you as you seek His guidance in every aspect of your life.

Prayer: Heavenly Father, today I seek Your divine guidance in my decision-making. I acknowledge You as the source of all wisdom and place my trust in Your knowledge of what is best for me. Help me not to rely on my understanding but on Your leading in every area of my life. Grant me wisdom and discernment as I navigate choices and challenges. Reveal Your will and guide me along the path You have prepared. In Jesus' name, I pray. Amen.

Day 30: Reflecting God's Light

Reflect on your role as a reflection of God's light in the world
Read Matthew 5, focusing on verses 14-16
Pray for the strength to shine God's light in your words and actions

As we conclude our 30-day devotion journey, let's reflect on our role as bearers of God's light in the world. In the midst of life's busyness, we often forget our calling to embody His love and grace.

Today, let's meditate on Matthew 5:14-16:

"You are the world's light. A city on a hill cannot be hidden. Nor do people light a lamp and put it under a basket. They put it on a lampstand, and it lights up the entire home. Allow your light to shine before others so that they can notice your good acts and worship your heavenly Father."

Consider the relevance of the following words: We are the world's light! We cannot hide the light that God has placed inside us, just as a city on a hill cannot be hidden. It is intended to radiate and influence others around us.

Consider how you've been expressing God's light through your words and actions. Were there times when fear or doubt dimmed that light? Identify areas for improvement and become more intentional about reflecting His love and grace.

While meditating on this, pray for the strength and courage to shine God's light brightly. Ask Him to daily fill you with His Spirit, empowering you to manifest His love, kindness, and mercy through your words and deeds.

Take a moment today to consider how you can intentionally illuminate God's light in your daily life. May His light guide your actions, bringing glory to His name.

Prayer: Heavenly Father, thank You for appointing me as a beacon of Your light in this world. Help me embrace this calling daily and let Your love and grace radiate through me. Forgive me for the moments when fear or doubt concealed Your light. Strengthen me, Lord, and fill me with Your Spirit, so I can boldly shine Your light in every situation. Grant me the wisdom to recognise opportunities to manifest Your love and goodness in my interactions with others. May my words and deeds glorify You and draw others closer to Your heart. Amen.

Conclusion:

Congratulations on completing this transformative 30-day devotional journey! Your achievement brings me genuine joy. I sincerely hope that the profound experiences you've had with God and Jesus during this period will remain a lasting wellspring of inspiration, continually shaping and elevating your faith.

Understanding that your relationship with God is an ongoing odyssey of growth and intimacy is paramount. To nurture this intimacy connection, remain steadfast in your dedication through prayer, diligent study of His Word, nurturing fellowship with fellow believers, and selfless service to those around you. By anchoring yourself deeply in Him, your faith will not only flourish but also usher in His abundant blessings into your life.

My heartfelt prayer is that God showers you with boundless blessings as you continue to walk hand in hand with Him, fervently seeking His divine guidance and selflessly sharing His love with the world. May your life shine brightly with His light, and may His grace and peace continually embrace you. Always remember to continue nurturing your faith, knowing that He is steadfastly by your side, guiding every step you take.

Sending you my warmest wishes for continued blessings and profound growth on your remarkable journey with Him!

Repeatable : Anchored in Faith: 30-Day Bible verses

Day 1: Embracing God's Promises
Isaiah 41:10 - "So do not fear, for I am with you; do not be dismayed, for I am your God. I will strengthen you and help you; I will uphold you with my righteous right hand."

Day 2: Trusting in God's Provision
Philippians 4:19 - "And my God will meet all your needs according to the riches of his glory in Christ Jesus."

Day 3: Casting Your Anxieties on Him
1 Peter 5:7 - "Cast all your anxiety on him because he cares for you."

Day 4: Finding Peace in God's Presence
Psalm 46:10 - "Be still, and know that I am God; I will be exalted among the nations, I will be exalted in the earth."

Day 5: The Power of Prayer
Philippians 4:6-7 - "Do not be anxious about anything, but in every situation, by prayer and petition, with thanksgiving, present your requests to God. And the peace of God, which transcends all understanding, will guard your hearts and your minds in Christ Jesus."

Day 6: Surrendering Control to God
Proverbs 3:5-6 - "Trust in the Lord with all your heart and lean not on your own understanding; in all your ways submit to him, and he will make your paths straight."

Day 7: Cultivating a Grateful Heart
1 Thessalonians 5:18 - "Give thanks in all circumstances; for this is God's will for you in Christ Jesus."

Day 8: Overcoming Fear with Faith
Psalm 34:4 - "I sought the Lord, and he answered me; he delivered me from all my fears."

Day 9: Renewing Your Mind
Romans 12:2 - "Do not conform to the pattern of this world, but be transformed by the renewing of your mind. Then you will be able to test and approve what God's will is—his good, pleasing and perfect will."

Day 10: Resting in God's Grace
2 Corinthians 12:9 - "But he said to me, 'My grace is sufficient for you, for my power is made perfect in weakness.' Therefore, I will boast all the more gladly about my weaknesses so that Christ's power may rest on me."

Day 11: Finding Strength in Weakness
Isaiah 40:29 - "He gives strength to the weary and increases the power of the weak."

Day 12: Seeking Wise Counsel
Proverbs 11:14 - "For lack of guidance, a nation falls, but victory is won through many advisers."

Day 13: Nurturing Healthy Relationships
Ecclesiastes 4:9-10 - "Two are better than one, because they have a good return for their labor: If either of them falls down, one can help the other up. But pity anyone who falls and has no one to help them up."

Day 14: Embracing Self-Care as a Spiritual Practice
1 Corinthians 6:19-20 - "Do you not know that your bodies are temples of the Holy Spirit, who is in you, whom you have received from God? You are not your own; you were bought at a price. Therefore, honor God with your bodies."

Day 15: Letting Go of Perfectionism
Psalm 139:14 - "I praise you because I am fearfully and wonderfully made; your works are wonderful, I know that full well."

Day 16: Embracing God's Timing
Ecclesiastes 3:1 - "There is a time for everything and a season for every activity under the heavens."

Day 17: Walking in God's Light
Psalm 119:105 - "Your word is a lamp for my feet, a light on my path."

Day 18: Living a Life of Purpose
Jeremiah 29:11 - "For I know the plans I have for you," declares the Lord, "plans to prosper you and not to harm you, plans to give you hope and a future."

Day 19: Holding on to Hope
Romans 15:13 - "May the God of hope fill you with all joy and peace as you trust in him, so that you may overflow with hope by the power of the Holy Spirit."

Day 20: Building a Strong Foundation in Christ
Matthew 7:24-25 - "Therefore everyone who hears these words of mine and puts them into practice is like a wise man who built his house on the

rock. The rain came down, the streams rose, and the winds blew and beat against that house; yet it did not fall because it had its foundation on the rock."

Day 21: Cultivating a Spirit of Contentment
Philippians 4:11-12 - "I am not saying this because I am in need, for I have learned to be content whatever the circumstances. I know what it is to be in need, and I know what it is to have plenty. I have learned the secret of being content in any and every situation, whether well fed or hungry, whether living in plenty or in want."

Day 22: Finding Comfort in the Psalms
Psalm 34:17 - "The righteous cry out, and the Lord hears them; he delivers them from all their troubles."

Day 23: Practising Mindfulness in God's Presence
Psalm 46:1 - "God is our refuge and strength, an ever-present help in trouble."

Day 24: Seeking Peace in Silence and Solitude
Psalm 62:1-2 - "Truly, my soul finds rest in God; my salvation comes from him. Truly, he is my rock and my salvation; he is my fortress, I will never be shaken."

Day 25: Extending Compassion to Yourself and Others
Colossians 3:12 - "Therefore, as God's chosen people, holy and dearly loved, clothe yourselves with compassion, kindness, humility, gentleness, and patience."

Day 26: Strengthening Your Faith Through Community

Hebrews 10:24-25 - "And let us consider how we may spur one another on toward love and good deeds, not giving up meeting together, as some are in the habit of doing, but encouraging one another—and all the more as you see the Day approaching."

Day 27: Celebrating God's Faithfulness
Lamentations 3:22-23 - "Because of the Lord's great love, we are not consumed, for his compassions never fail. They are new every morning; great is your faithfulness."

Day 28: Embracing the Power of Forgiveness
Colossians 3:13 - "Bear with each other and forgive one another if any of you have a grievance against someone. Forgive as the Lord forgave you."

Day 29: Letting Go of Worry and Anxiety
Philippians 4:6-7 - "Do not be anxious about anything, but in every situation, by prayer and petition, with thanksgiving, present your requests to God. And the peace of God, which transcends all understanding, will guard your hearts and your minds in Christ Jesus."

Day 30: Embracing God's Unconditional Love
Romans 8:38-39 - "For I am convinced that neither death nor life, neither angels nor demons, neither the present nor the future, nor any powers, neither height nor depth, nor anything else in all creation, will be able to separate us from the love of God that is in Christ Jesus our Lord."

Conclusion:
As you journey through these 30 days, remember that God is with you every step of the way. May His Word guide you, His love comfort you, and His Spirit empower you to overcome anxiety and experience the abundant life

He has promised. Take these devotions to heart, reflect on them, and apply them to your life, trusting that God will transform your anxious heart into one filled with peace, joy, and hope. May you be forever anchored in your faith and find rest in the loving arms of our Savior, Jesus Christ. Amen.

"My sheep hear my voice, and I know them, and they follow me: and I give unto them eternal life; and they shall never perish, neither shall any man pluck them out of my hand." - John 10:27-28

The Four Spiritual Laws:

God loves you deeply and has a beautiful plan for your life.

Acknowledge that sin has created a separation between you and God.

Jesus Christ is the only bridge to reconciling you with God.

To experience this reconciliation, you need to personally accept Jesus Christ as your Savior and Lord.

The Prayer of Repentance:

Gracious God, thank you for all your blessings, even though I am undeserving. I come to You humbly to ask for forgiveness for my sins. Please cleanse me of my wrongdoings and guide me back to Your path. I am grateful for Your constant love and attention. Please continue to bless me with Your grace and mercy. I will strive to live my life in a way that brings honor and glory to You. Amen

Both the Four Spiritual Laws and the Prayer of Repentance serve as tools to express one's genuine repentance, embrace Jesus Christ, and embark on a personal and transformative relationship with Him. It's important to recognize that these expressions are not rigid formulas but sincere reflections of faith and surrender. If you rededicate your life to Jesus for a fresh start/beginning, congratulations to you. If any of you have followed and said the sinner's prayer to give your life to Jesus for the first time, please be advised to attend your local churches. If you have any queries, please feel free to contact me: **karynleechua5784@gmail.com / connect@karyninternational.com**

Here are more Bible verses that encourage calling out to Jesus in any of your situations. God is omnipresent, He hears our cry (prayers) :

Bible verses on unconditional Love 🩶 of God :

Let's take a closer look at each of these verses and their significance in understanding the unconditional love of Jesus:

1. Romans 5:8 - "But God demonstrates his own love for us in this: While we were still sinners, Christ died for us."

    In this verse, the apostle Paul reminds us that God's love is not dependent on our actions or worthiness. Even when we were still sinners, separated from God, Jesus willingly died on the cross for our sins. This demonstrates the depth of God's love for us - a love that is undeserved and unconditional.

2. John 3:16 - "For God so loved the world that he gave his one and only Son, that whoever believes in him shall not perish but have eternal life."

    This is one of the most well-known verses in the Bible and encapsulates the heart of God's love for humanity. It explains that God's love is so immense that he sent his only Son, Jesus, into the world to save us. This act of sacrifice and love is a demonstration of God's unconditional love, as it offers the opportunity for anyone who believes in Jesus to have eternal life.

3. Ephesians 2:4-5 - "But because of his great love for us, God, who is rich in mercy, made us alive with Christ even when we were dead in transgressions—it is by grace you have been saved."

These verses emphasize God's abundant mercy and love for us. Although we were dead in our sins, deserving of punishment, God, out of his great love, made us alive with Christ. This passage highlights the fact that our salvation is entirely dependent on God's grace and love, rather than any merit or effort on our part.

4. 1 John 4:9-10 - "This is how God showed his love among us: He sent his one and only Son into the world that we might live through him. This is love: not that we loved God, but that he loved us and sent his Son as an atoning sacrifice for our sins."
    Here, John describes the ultimate expression of God's love for us. He sent his Son as an atoning sacrifice for our sins, reconciling us to himself. This sacrifice demonstrates that God's love is not conditional upon our love for Him, but rather on his love for us. It is a love that seeks our redemption and restoration, despite our imperfections.

5. 1 John 4:16 - "So we have come to know and to believe the love that God has for us. God is love, and anyone who abides in love abides in God, and God abides in them."

6. Galatians 2:20 - "I have been crucified with Christ and I no longer live, but Christ lives in me. The life I now live in the body, I live by faith in the Son of God, who loved me and gave himself for me."

7. Psalm 23:4 - "Yea, though I walk through the valley of the shadow of death,
    I will fear no evil, for You *are* with me; Your rod and Your staff comfort me."

8. Psalm 37:3 - "Trust in the LORD, and do good; dwell in the land, and feed on His faithfulness."

    These verses reassure us that when we abide in love, we are abiding in God, because God is love. It reminds us that God's very nature is love, and that love is an integral part of our relationship with him. Through Jesus' perfect example and the gift of his unconditional love, we can experience a deep connection with God and reflect that love on others.

Closing Prayer: Let Your Light Shine Through Us

In the quiet corners of our hearts, let us offer this prayer as a closing benediction, a sacred whisper that resonates with the essence of our shared journey:

Lord, as we conclude this transformative odyssey, we humbly beseech you: Shine your light on us today. Illuminate our minds with wisdom, our hearts with compassion, and our souls with unwavering faith. Through us, dear Heavenly Father, shine your light. Make us instruments of your peace, channels of your love, and reflections of your boundless grace. Guide our hands to heal, our words to soothe, and our actions to inspire.

In this sacred moment, cleanse our hearts, O Lord. Purify our intentions, rid us of any malice, and fill us with the purest love. Make us vessels of your divine purpose, vessels that carry your transformative message to every corner of the world. With this prayer, we surrender our fears, our doubts, and our inadequacies. In their place, bestow upon us the strength to carry your light bravely, the wisdom to share it generously, and the humility to recognize it in others. May this prayer echo beyond these pages, becoming a beacon of hope and love for all who seek your divine presence. In your holy name, we conclude, Amen.

"I will restore to you the years that the swarming locust has eaten, the hopper, the destroyer, and the cutter. The great army sent among you." - Joel 2:25

"For I know the thoughts that I think toward you, says the LORD, thoughts of peace and not of evil, to give you a future and a hope." - Jeremiah 29:11

"For the word of God *is* living and powerful, and sharper than any two-edged sword, piercing even to the division of soul and spirit, and of joints and marrow, and is a discerner of the thoughts and intents of the heart." - Hebrews 4:12

"For God so loved the world that He gave His only begotten Son, that whoever believes in Him should not perish but have everlasting life." - John 3:16

Read: The Whole Armor of God in Ephesians 6:10-18

Acknowledgments:

To Jesus who loves the world:

I dedicate this book, "Why Jesus? Navigating His Transformative Message" to you, Lord, with heartfelt gratitude for Your endless love, guidance, and inspiration.

To my beloved family

Your unwavering support for this book has made it better in countless ways. Your presence in my life is a testament to God's blessings.

To all who shared their personal testimonies:

Your heartfelt stories have enriched the pages of this book, showcasing the profound impact of faith and adding depth to its message. Your courage and honesty inspire us all.

With profound thanks and deep love,

Karyn Chua
www.karyninternational.com

ABOUT THE AUTHOR

A Christ follower who experienced Jesus' love at the age of 11, Karyn L. Chua came from a small charming tin mining town of Kampar in Perak, West Malaysia. However, her life's trajectory deviated drastically when she was given away at birth. Believing that it was God leading and guiding her, even at a tender age, she came into the care of a compassionate woman who graciously welcomed her into her heart and home. Through her benevolence, Karyn received invaluable gifts, including that of education, a blessing that eventually led her to Singapore in 1976 and later to Australia in 1983, where she completed a business course.

In the intricate fabric of her life, a turning point materialised in 1995 when she encountered a Bible-walking man, who knew the Bible from front to back, embodying his faith. Their subsequent marriage marked the commencement of a shared odyssey. His profession whisked them to various corners of the world, enabling them to immerse themselves in diverse cultures and embrace the essence of international living.

Her journey has brought her back to Australia, where her children have found their paths and are diligently pursuing their careers. Meanwhile, her husband continues his work overseas. Together, they navigate the delicate equilibrium of a life shaped by myriad of experiences and global connections.

www.ingramcontent.com/pod-product-compliance
Lightning Source LLC
Chambersburg PA
CBHW071427090426
42737CB00011B/1594